REPRESENTING TRIBE

About the Author

Dr Asoka Kumar Sen taught history at Tata College Chaibasa, West Singhbhum from where he retired as University Professor in 2002. He is presently an independent researcher of tribal history. Besides authoring *The Educated Middle Class and Indian Nationalism, Bengali Intelligentsia and Popular Uprisings 1855-73* and *Wilkinson's Rules: Context, Content and Ramifications* (ed.) he has contributed research papers to several national and international conferences as well as journals and edited books including the forthcoming volume entitled *The British Empire and the Natural World: Environmental Encounters in South Asia* published by the Oxford University Press. Dr. Sen was awarded a short fellowship by the Department of Sociology, Delhi School of Economics. He had also the distinction of working as a Researcher for Sussex University, UK on the British Academy Project entitled: *The East India Company and the Natural World: Environment, Innovation and Ideas at the Core of the British Empire* during December 2005 June 2007. He is presently the editor of *Manwa Katha*, a Journal published by the *Ashin Dasgupta Institute of Tribal History*, Kolkata.

Representing Tribe

The Ho of Singhbhum under Colonial Rule

ASOKA KUMAR SEN

CONCEPT PUBLISHING COMPANY PVT. LTD.
NEW DELHI-110059

ISBN-13: 978-81-8069-753-1

First Published 2011

Published and Printed by

Concept Publishing Company Pvt. Ltd.
Regd. Office:
A/15-16, Commercial Block, Mohan Garden
New Delhi-110059 (India)
Phones : 25351460, 25351794, *Fax* : 091-11-25357109
Email : publishing@conceptpub.com
Website: www.conceptpub.com

Cataloging in Publication Data--*Courtesy:* D.K. Agencies (P) Ltd. <docinfo@dkagencies.com>

Sen, Asoka Kumar.
Representing tribe: the Ho of Singhbhum under colonial rule / Asoka Kumar Sen.
p. cm.
Includes bibliographical references (p.) and index.
ISBN 9788180697531

1. Ho (Indic people)--Government policy--India--Singhbhūm. 2. Ho (Indic people) -India--Singhbhūm--Social conditions. 3. India--History--British occupation, 1765-1947. I. Title.

DDC 305.89595 22

To

My Father

Sunil Kumar Sen

(1914 – 1984)

who inspired me into Tribal History

Preface

The essays included in this book were written over a decade which took a few more years to revise and thread together under one cover. In fact when I was writing the essays the idea of a book was not in my mind. Later I found that these had a broad unity relating a particular *Adivasi* community, the Ho, and the district where they are concentrated. To historicize them was kind of paying back the debt to the soil I was born. It no less served the contemporary urge among the indigenes to rightfully situate them in mainstream history. In doing so I was merely extending the tradition of reconstructing *Adivasi* history initiated more than half a century before. But instead of thematizing anti-British tribal movements I decided to explore new areas that portrayed the more mundane and regular with which their life was made. However, the correspondences, reports and ethnographies that researchers usually draw on did not provide necessary details. Task became all the more difficult because of the absence of an oral tradition relating the past of the Ho. At this point my long researches at the District Record Room Chaibasa provided necessary information that helped reconstruct a more intimate and 'true' story of Ho life.

This representation needed another shift by putting both the ethnographic and anthropological conceptualizations of the tribe under scanner and contending the notion of the indigene as both a changeless and colonially constructed community. While doing so I was in fact landing myself into trouble by titling the book as Representing the Tribe and interchangeably using the expressions tribe, indigene and *Adivasi.* I understand that it is problematic to do so because the term 'tribe' is a contested one for its derogatory connotation. On the other hand, the other two are often not found historically tenable. Yet I chose to invoke all three words in tandem not only because these denoted the same ethnic group, in the present case the Ho, but also because these had historic and contemporary significance. Tribe is used in colonial records along with its antonyms aboriginals and autochthones, to denote the historic specificities of indigenous groups. Moreover, prefixed by scheduled, this word represents their constitutional status in India also. On the other hand, the other two are preferred by indigenes as the appropriate name by which they want themselves to be addressed, a fact we cannot ignore when we seek to historicize them.

I owe a deep sense of gratitude to many without whose support and help this work would not have been possible. First it goes to the publishers of those journals where some of the earlier versions of the essays contained in this book appeared. These include *History* (Journal of Burdwan University), where the eighth and fifth essays were published in Vol. II, No. I, 1999 and Vol. VI, No. I, 2003 respectively and *South Asia* : Journal of South Asian Studies, n.s., Vol. XXVII, No. I, April 2004 for the sixth. I am grateful to Ashin Dasgupta Institute of Tribal History, Kolkata for the use of the second essay, which was Ashin Dasgupta Memorial Lecture delivered by me on 31 October 1999. Thanks are due to Dr. Mrs. Padmaja Sen, Reader, Dept. of Philosophy, Mahila College, Chaibasa for kindly allowing me to include Roughsedge's Equation, of which she is the co-author, in this volume.

I am grateful to late Father Mathew Areeparampil, then Director, Tribal Research and Training Centre, Lupungutu for extending library facilities to me. For valuable study materials I remain grateful to Prof. Gautam Bhadra, Dr. Ritambhara Hebbar, Dr. Barbara Verardo, Dr. Padmanabha Samarendra, Dr. Sangeeta Dasgupta and finally to Fr. J. Cutinha for materials from London. I would like to extend thanks to my old colleagues at Tata College, Chaibasa Sri H.M.L. Baxi and Sri S.S. Mohanty for their encouragement and assistance. I am extremely grateful to my colleague Dr. D.N. Mahto for preparing the maps and Sri P.K. Ray for providing the photo-copy of Ratneshvar Roy's Tour Diary and other materials on him. I have no words to offer my sincere thanks to Dr. Mahesh Rangarajan, Prof. Richard Grove and Dr. Vinita Damodaran for their gestures of help. Dr. Somnath Roy, former Prof. & Head, Dept. of History, Burdwan University has always been a source of profound inspiration to me. I am thankful to my friends at the District Record Room, Chaibasa Dr. Mrs. Meena Kumari, then the Archives Officer, and Late Lakhindar Das for their tremendous support and help. For photographs, I am thankful to Sri Nirmal Sarkar of Gem Studio, Chaibasa and

Sri Ramesh Jerai, Johar, Chaibasa. I thank Sri Manish Kumar Singh and Sri Sudipta Nandy for their valuable assistance.

I am grateful to Shri Ashok Mittal of the Concept Publishing Company Pvt. Ltd., New Delhi for kindly publishing my work.

My mother Mrs. Bela Sen and my wife Padmaja made a happy home where pursuing research work was more than a pleasure. My daughters Purba and Ishita, sons-in-law Rishi and Sourabh and above all Soumya, my grand daughter, brought rare moments of joy, which never allowed my research interests to flag. My labour will be amply rewarded by the joy this book may bring to all of them.

Chaibasa **Asoka Kumar Sen**
16 February, 2009

Contents

Abbreviations

AGRCD	Annual General Report Chotanagpur Division
CN	Collection No.
CS	Craven Settlement
DC's Office	Deputy Commissioner's (Singhbhum) Office
DR	Diku Report
DRRC	District Record Room Chaibasa
FL	Fly Leaf
FN	File No.
FS	File Serial
GAR	General Administration Report
GD	General Department
LRAR	Land Revenue Administration Report, Singhbhum
PLJR	Patna Law Journal Reports
RB	Revenue Branch
SWFPDR	South West Frontier Political Despatch Register
TD	Tour Diary of Ratneshvar Roy
TS	Tuckey Settlement
TSKP	Tuckey Settlement Khuntkatti Papers
TSVN	Tuckey Settlement Village Note
VN	Vasta (Bag) No.

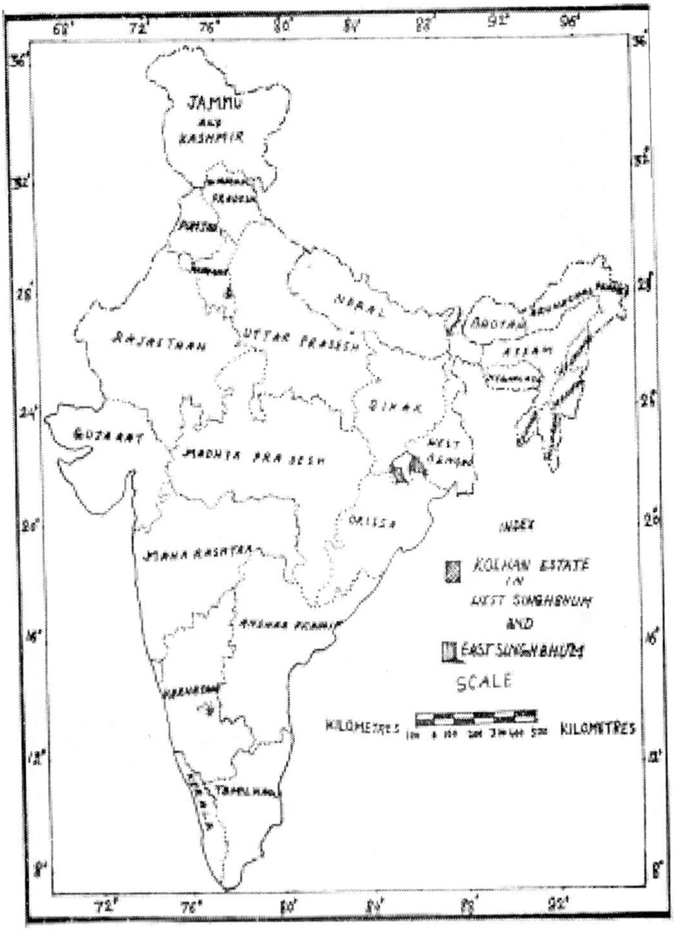
JAMMU
AND
KASHMIR
RAJASTHAN
UTTAR PRADESH
NEPAL
BHUTAN
ASSAM
BIHAR
GUJARAT
MADHYA PRADESH
WEST
BENGAL
ORISSA
MAHA RASHTRA
ANDHRA PRADESH
TAMIL NADU
INDEX
KOLHAN ESTATE
IN
WEST SINGHBHUM
AND
EAST SINGHBHUM
SCALE
KILOMETRES
KILOMETRES

JHARKHAND
GODDA
PAKUR
KODARMA
DEOGARH
GIRIDIH
DUMKA
PALAMAU
CHATRA
GARHWA
HAZARIBAGH
JAMTARA
DHANBAD
LATEHAR
BOKARO
LOHARDAGA
GUMLA
RANCHI
SARAIKELA-KHARSAWAN
SIMDEGA
WEST SINGHBHUM
EAST SINGHBHUM

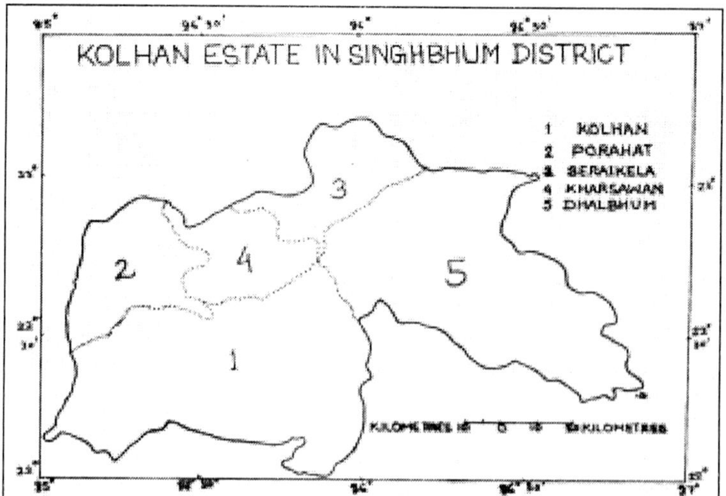
KOLHAN ESTATE IN SINGHBHUM DISTRICT
1 KOLHAN
2 PORAHAT
3 SERAIKELA
4 KHARSAWAN
5 DHALBHUM
1
2
3
4
5

1

Introduction

Representing Tribe[1] historicizes pre-independence Ho tribe of Singhbhum district[2], the principal demographic group inhabiting its Kolhan region. Tribal identity assertion today claims rightful spaces not only in polity, socio-economy and culture but also in the mainstream episteme. The basic question however is: what is tribal episteme itself and what should be the right modality of appropriating their past. To study 'tribes' is to be drawn into the world of colonial knowledge. British ethnography is part of the discourse commonly known as Orientalism. But one has to understand that, even in their oneness, Indian orientalism and tribal orientalism had a major difference. When Indian orientalism was reconstructed, scholars at the Asiatic Society of Bengal could draw upon literate and archaeological sources. But when it came to dealing with tribal society, British administrator-ethnographers as well as Indian scholars were generally forced to make do with oral traditions and their observations of lived reality as their main sources of information. This information was saturated by ideologically structured tribal epistemology.

British ethnography on the Ho of Jharkhand (as with other major *Adivasi* groups like the Munda, Santal and Oraon) has distinct features. First, it was closely linked with the depth of colonial penetration of the region. And next, the epistemic quest of the imperialists was not simply to seek knowledge for its own sake. It was rather, to use Said's famous phrase, part of their 'technology of power'. The relationship between the Occident and the Orient (the tribal orient in this case) was therefore a relationship of domination, more accurately, of a complex hegemony.[3] As a result British ethnography merely focused on selected and administratively 'useful' aspects of indigenous life.

Repeated uncritically by later ethnographers, often verbatim, this fund of information structured an inadequate popular official literature[4], which has left its mark on the ethnography and anthropology of the region.

Ho studies began more or less in the wake of the centenary of the revolt of 1857. Beginning with K.K. Datta[5] the trend set in of producing a nationalist literature incorporating resistance movements by the *Adivasis* of Bihar perhaps to show that anti-Britishism was truly national. Anti-British indigenous movements became therefore the patent theme inspiring studies[6] by J.C. Jha, C P. Singh, M. Sahu, N. Sur, Gautam Bhadra, Sanjukta Das Gupta and S.K. Sen. Of them Jha and Sur recalled Ho uprising as part of Chotanagpur struggle while Bhadra did so within a much broader locale. Singh and Sahu perhaps set the trend of historicizing Ho material and moral culture also in some details, though we do not find Sahu's comprehensiveness in Singh who studied only up to 1832. In fact, D.N. Majumdar had pioneered the study of Ho culture long before them.[7] But the lack of history in Majumdar and generalized studies of Singh and Sahu render their texts rather descriptive and flat. To take a single instance their uprising-narrative is more or less cause-consequence-centric, which fail to apprehend the whole range of politics.[8]

Fortunately about the same time we notice the construction of another genre of writings, which was approach-wise and thematically diverse. More prolific is the demographic interaction, mainly Rajputisation of tribe, rather Hindu influence on them[9], by S. Sinha, K.S. Singh, M. Areeparampil, B.B. Chaudhuri, and Sinha, Sen and Panchabhai. On the other hand, search for cultural identity[10] among the Ho of Singhbhum is addressed by P.C. Hembram and P.K. Dasgupta.

Scholars have also focused on other themes related to the *Adivasis* of Chotanagpur. Economy of this region is variously studied.[11] Two essays by P.P. Mohapatra investigate the land and credit market and agrarian question. Areeparampil highlights land alienation and forest rights in his papers. A.K. Srivastava's study is on the coal mining industry in Chotanagpur in the pan-Indian context. Thematic variety[12] is provided again when M.P. Yorke's empirical study details the decision-making process among the Ho, A.K. Sen (ed.) takes up Wilkinson's civil rules in the historical and contemporary context and M. Kishwar probes gender problem in Ho society in her series of essays. S.S. Sinha extends the discussion on gender by studying 'the intricate connections between gender, patriarchy, colonialism and constructions of witches in adivasi societies of Chotanagpur.'[13]

More recent engagement of scholars however is to ecologically study indigenous space, both physical and cultural, highlighting their attitude to such natural objects as *Jal*, *Jungle* and *Jameen* as also colonial government's policies towards these. Of the more recent we can particularly name the studies by K. Sivaramkrishnan and Vinita Damodaran. While studying statist intervention in effecting environmental change in colonial eastern India the former[14] thematises forested landscape of Chotanagpur, including Singhbhum. On the other hand, Damodaran 'explore(s) the plateau as an economic, ethnic, anthropologic, religious, and ecological terrain'.[15] Against this grain more spatio-demographically specific is another work that historicizes conflict and collaboration of Ho and colonial ecological perceptions leading to Ho social protest.[16]

The above diachronic and synchronic accounts however suffer from some broad limitations. First, mostly (except Areeparampil's essay on socio-religious life, Hembram, Dasgupta, Yorke, Sen and Kishwar) the focus is on the broader canvas of Chotanagpur or select tribal groups (Chaudhuri, Sinha, Singh, Areeparampil on mines and Sinha *et al.*) where Singhbhum and the Ho are either missing or remain neglected. Next, some of the studies on the Ho and Singhbhum (Chaudhuri, Areeparampil, Majumdar, Sinha, Hembram, Dasgupta, Sinha *et al.* and Yorke) are either ahistorical or inadequately historical.

It is not however the lack of focus alone that has inspired this narrative. It is rather the very notion of text making in the above diachronic writings that I seek to examine and critique. Textuality here clings more or less to the structuralist tradition of literary texts conveying stable meanings by arriving at definite and final conclusions. This stability conducts itself within hierarchization of resources to draw upon. I believe that there is an essential link between place from which information has originated and information itself. Resources here largely concern, which I prefer to term, elite archives of Delhi, the national capital, Kolkata and Patna, the provincial capitals. Elitism lies, besides their administrative significance, in the lopsided corpus they generate conforming to the colonial ideology of the peripheries existing for the metropolis. Consequently, provinces and districts stand emasculated and expunged from national and provincial discourses and villages, the basic constituting units, from all these.[17]

The result is both lack of information as well as prevalence virtually of a culture of misinformation. This is understandably the product of the belief in the sanctity of the archival evidence of the select category stated above. When this evidence is accepted more or less on their face value misconceived generalizations follow largely in diachronic writings. Grounded on the above conclusions synchronic approach often tends to be somewhat inauthentic. The net result is putative understanding of the intervened community as well as the region and the production of a whole genre of tentative and often tainted writing.

The present work does not, however, intend to reconstruct a comprehensive counter narrative of Singhbhum and Ho but by critiquing the priority of the stock of meanings offers a more open ended narrative. To do this, I, however, do not draw on trans-archival resources[18] but seek to work, on the one hand, within the archives to expose the latent contradictions. On the other, I contend the capability of easily approachable elite archives (national and state-level) to adequately epistomize regions. This necessitates an archaeological movement down into the more basement level of the District Archives where information about the district as a region and villages as its components are more elaborate and intimate. With this data bank we can perhaps examine for the time being the existing historical and empirical findings and tread newer furrows to more fruitfully illuminate the region and the people under review.

The first essay nutshells the physical, cultural and human geography of the space under study and also the historical setting against which the essays have been mainly drawn.

The second seeks to more or less delineate the boundary of existing historiography and to emphasize that over-dependence on and an uncritical study of archival materials available at national and state capitals had rendered the projections rather distorted and incomplete. While identifying some of the major stereotypes it calls for other minor but distracting ones to be questioned. This way I broadly question the imaging of Ho indigenes in the colonial ethnography and often post-colonial reconstruction heavily drawing on it. This reimaging when supplemented by my other writings[19] may perhaps clarify that my representation of the Ho is the sum of this critique of colonial reading and the assertion of the self-image by the Ho.

The third essay continues the questioning through an analytical methodology not generally deployed by a student of history. But the invocation of this approach is to underline that in evaluating historical facts, more so facts from archival records, the reading should be more intense so that we are able to comprehend the bias and prejudices latent in them. This is particularly necessary as we historicize a subaltern community.

The next essay focuses on additional genealogy of historical knowledge with the help of a private collection. This in fact is an official report preserved by the family to which the author belonged rather than a private paper of the class of a private diary or correspondence or memoir or biography. But this collection becomes an inescapable source material for the richness of data, that may inspire researchers to look for similar such sources in order to study regional histories. The information as recollected in this volume has also another purpose to serve. It involves the process of how the biography of the author, whom his family members did not remember in precise details, should be reconstructed. Ratneshvar of this essay was a Hindu by faith, which precluded any information about him from the local Church papers. Nor could we derive any information from the local municipality due to the absence then of the practice of recording birth. So to retrieve the man from near oblivion was a challenging task. The experience was thrilling to discover his date of birth in a file of the Permanent Establishment, or to stumble on his first application for job or other papers containing details of his service career. I have the feeling that a researcher has often to play the Sherlock Holmes[20] to meet the demands of local history. But while historically discovering the man and his family I was also perhaps grappling with the contemporary historical ambience. As such Ratneshvar from this detection emerged not simply as an individual but also as the representative of an inchoate social category of educated middle class. In a remote town of Singhbhum the extension of this culture is no less a significant phenomenon for a future research on the emergence and role of Ho intelligentsia in public life.[21]

While the above essays more or less critique the bias involved in historical raw material and offer an additional source the remaining ones seek to understand how through a changed technology a region or its demography may be more meaningfully mediated. While studying the Ho of Singhbhum we find their pre-British past virtually effaced and the colonial period brought into limelight. We have outlived the days of dynastic and elitist approaches[22], more so to look at the bottom cursorily from top and without, and that too with uncritical use of colonial-day recordings preserved at centralized places. If instead we make a humble beginning with a focus on tribal life itself and try to collate additional resources we will perhaps be able to move in the right direction. My studies of the vast body of Village Papers, which accommodated oral evidences, as also other sources make me dare that perhaps light may yet streak through layers of ignorance. The potentiality of the resources are amply borne out by the next three essays which appropriate additional information to question the inept image of the indigenes in synchronic writings and offer a more intimate knowledge about a region and oral societies in general.

More popular assumption about Ho culture[23] often tends to be ahistorical. First is that Ho society has had been homogenous and egalitarian. Second is that the society was able to evolve customs, which were more or less stable and general. And lastly, tribal economy dependent on agriculture, products of jungle, barter system and frugality of wants was both self-containing and self-sustaining. These notions also argue for the distinct indigenous (Ho in the present case) identity as different from others and basic impregnability of their collective life. For a researcher these can form hypothetical beginning points. In fact, as we grapple with the historical evidences rather uncritically we are misled to believe that the British in fact inherited certain fixed traditions, which they thankfully reinforced. While we are aware that there are some elements of truth, perhaps it is time to examine how true these basic assumptions are, not however with the aim of dismantling the notion of tribe but to historically re-mantle and reinstate it. It is because we cannot remain oblivious of the impact of British political economy, and for that matter the entire stretch of pre-colonial period, which made and re-made Ho society from its base.[24] This created fissures in the society, remaking social attitudes and behaviour and bringing change in their original homogenous order and with it their notion of self. This reality stands revealed by last three essays.

The first questions the continuity of a homogenous and egalitarian tribal framework and seeks to underline that slow but irreversible current of change was in operation from pre-British past itself. The next foregrounds the reality of gender assertion for greater space in social life to which the society had to respond as well as the areas of disempowerment that had been growing with male hold increasing over time. The ebbing egalitarianism and gender assertion were evidently signs of a community in internal ferment. The last grapples with the enveloping Jharkhand phenomenon of labour migrations caused by the contradictions within indigenous socio-economy as well as the encouragement of colonial forces for which tribal labour market was a haven for the flourishing tea industry of Assam. The picture that presents itself is that of a community placed at a strange crossroad of history. These details conflict with the stereotype of a contented and happy tribe, which the benign British rule delivered and which broadly constituted the subject matter of the statist discourse we generally come across. To provide these details I first configure the spatio-demographic and historical environment of Singhbhum.

NOTES

1. I owe a clarification about the structuration of this work. It examines two broad ideas, first the existing corpus of a text to represent the Ho and the other its reconstruction. Though the term text presupposes a literary work or its main body under a title and written by one or more authors, the entire corpus of Ho historiography represented by an ensemble of books as well as essays, physically constituting not one but many texts, has been used as a singular like in a common noun unified by their commonality of discourse about a certain place and people. The work critically examines this historiographic corpus and then seeks to move beyond it in order to reconstruct Ho history. The notion of text and textuality has been studied on the basis of T. Eagleton, *Literary Theory*, Basil Blackwell, (Oxford, 1990) (1983); G. C. Spivak, *Jacques Derrida of Grammatology*, Motilal Banarsidass, (Delhi, 1994), (1976), Editor's Preface; J. Sturrrock, *Structuralism and Since from Levi Stauss to Derrida,* Oxford University Press, (Oxford, 1988) (1979); C. Norris, *Deconstuction, Theory and Practice*, Routledge, (London & New York, 1993), (1982).
2. Presently forming part of Jharkhand state the district is now divided into East and West Singhbhum as well as Seraikela-Kharsawan. The Hos live predominantly in West Singhbhum.
3. Edward Said, *Orientalism*, Harmondsworth: Penguin Books, 1985, pp. 4–5. For studying this link between knowledge and power in the Indian setting

one may also see B.S. Cohn, *Colonialism and its Forms of Knowledge*, Oxford University Press, (Delhi, 1997), pp. ix, 4.

4. Lt. S.R. Tickell, 'Memoir on the Ho Desum (Improperly Called Kolehan)', in *Journal of the Asiatic Society of Bengal*, Vol.XI, pt. I (1840); E.T. Dalton, *Tribal History of Eastern India*, Cosmo Publications, (Delhi 1973); J.A.Craven, *Final Report on the Settlement of Kolhan Government Estate 1897*, Bengal Secretariat Press, (Calcutta, 1898); L.S.S. O'Malley, *Bengal District Gazetteers: Singhbhum, Seraikela and Kharsawan,* The Bengal Secretariat Book Depot, (Calcutta, 1910); A.D. Tuckey, *Final Report on the Resettlement of the Kolhan Government Estate in the District of Singhbhum 1913-1918,* Superintendent, Government Printing, Bihar and Orissa, (Patna 1920).
5. 'Raja Arjun Singh of Porahat – the Popular Leader of Singhbhum during the Movement of 1857-59' in K.K. Datta (ed.), *Unrest Against British Rule in Bihar 1831-1859,* (Patna, 1957), pp. 66–76.
6. K.K. Datta, *Santal Insurrection of 1855-57,* University of Calcutta Press, (Calcutta, 1940); J.C. Jha, *Kol Insurrection in Chotanagpur*, (Calcutta, 1964); C.P. Singh, *The Ho Tribe of Singhbhum,* Classical Publications, (New Delhi, 1978); M. Sahu, *The Kolhan under the British Rule*, (Calcutta, 1985); N. Sur, 'Chotanagpur and the Rising of 1857', *Bengal Past and Present*, (January-December 1986), pp. 28-62; Gautam Bhadra, 'Four Rebels of Eighteen-Fifty Seven', in *Subaltern Studies IV*, Oxford University Press (OUP), (Delhi, 1990), (1985), pp. 257-263; Sanjukta Das Gupta, 'Rebellion in a Little Known District of the Empire', in Sabyasachi Bhattacharya (ed.) *Rethinking 1857*, Orient Longman, (New Delhi, 2007); S.K.Sen, *Tribal Struggle for Freedom: Singhbhum 1820-1858*, Concept Publishing Company Pvt. Ltd., (New Delhi, 2008).
7. D.N. Majumdar, *A Tribe in Transition: Study in Cultural Pattern*, Longmans Green & Co., Ltd., (Calcutta, 1937); *The Affairs of a Tribe*, (Calcutta, 1950).
8. I have in mind R. Guha, *Elementary Aspects of Peasant Insurgency in Colonial India*, OUP, (Delhi, 1983).
9. S. Sinha, 'State Formation and Rajput Myth in Tribal Central India', *Man in India*, Vol. 42, No. I, (March 1962), pp. 35–80; 'Tribe, Caste & Peasant Continua', *Man in India*, Vol. 45, No. I, (March 1965), pp. 57–83; K.S. Singh, 'State-Formation in Tribal Society: Some Preliminary Observations', *Journal of Indian Anthropological Society*, Vol. 6, (1971), pp. 161–181; M. Areeparampil, 'Socio-cultural and Religious Movements among the Ho Tribals of Singhbhum District of Bihar', in M. Miri (ed.), *Continuity and Change in Tribal Society*, Indian Institute of Advanced Study, (Shimla, 1993), pp. 396-436; B.B. Chaudhuri, 'Auponivesik Purba Bharate Hindu Adivasi Sanskritik Samparka', *Chaturanga,* (Magh 1401), (Jaistha 1402), (Bhadra 1403), (Pous 1403), (Shravan-Ashwin 1404); S.C. Sinha, J. Sen and S. Panchabhai, 'The Concept of Diku among the Tribes of Chotanagpur,' *Man in India*, Vol. 49, No. 2, (April-June 1969), pp. 122–38.

10. P.C. Hembram, 'Return to the Sacred Grove', in K.S. Singh (ed.), *Tribal Movements in India*, Vol. 2, (New Delhi, 1983), pp. 88-91; P.K. Dasgupta, 'The Adi Samaj Movement among the Ho', in K.S. Singh (ed.), *Tribal Movements*, pp. 93–107.
11. P.P. Mohapatra, 'Land and Credit Market in Chotanagpur 1880-1950', *Studies in History,* 6. 2. n.s., (1990), pp. 163-203; 'Class Conflict and Agrarian Regimes in Chotanagpur 1860-1950', *The Economic and Social History Review*, 28, 1 (1991), pp. 1-42; M. Areeparampil, 'Industies, Mines and Dispossession of Indigenous Peoples: The case of Chotanagpur', in W. Fernandes and E. Ganguly Thukral (eds.), Development, Displacement and Rehabilitation, *Indian Social Scientist*, (1989), pp. 14–38; 'Forest Policy and Denial of Tribal Rights', in W. Fernandes (ed.), *National Development and Tribal Deprivation*, Indian Social Institute, (New Delhi, 1992), pp. 148–74; A.K. Srivastava, *Coal Mining Industry in India*, (New Delhi, 1988).
12. M.P. Yorke, 'Decisions and Analogy: Political Structure and Discourse among the Ho Tribals of India', (unpublished Ph.D. thesis submitted to the School of Oriental and African Studies, University of London, October 1976); A.K. Sen (ed.), *Wilkinson's Rules: Context, Content and Ramifications,* Tata College, (Chaibasa, 1999); M. Kishwar, 'Toilng without Rights: Ho Women in Singhbhum', *Economic and Political Weekly*, 17, 24, 31 January (1987).
13. S.S. Sinha, 'Adivasis, Gender and the "Evil Eye": The Construction(s) of Witches in Colonial Chotanagpur', *The Indian Historical Review,* Volume XXXIII, Number 1 (January 2006), pp. 127–49.
14. S. Sivaramakrishnan, *Modern Forests: Statemaking and Environmental Changes in Colonial Eastern India*, OUP, (Delhi, 1999).
15. Vinita Damodaran, 'Indigenous Forests: Discourse, and Resistance in Chotanagpur, 1860-2002', in G. Cederlof & K. Sivaramakrishnan (eds.), *Ecological Nationalisms: Nature, Livelihoods, and Identities in South Asia*, Permanent Black, (Delhi, 2005), pp. 115–50.
16. A.K. Sen, 'Collaboration and Conflict; Environmental Legacies of the Ho of Kolhan (1700-1918),' Deepak Kumar, Vinita Damodaran & Rohan D'Souza (ed.) *The British Empire and the Natural World: Environmental Encounters in South Asia*. OUP, (New Delhi, forthcoming).
17. This is a general process, true also for the Ho. This has been studied in my essay 'Writing Local History and the District Record Room'. *Proceedings of the Indian Historical Records Commission*, 58th Session, 2003.
18. In fact colonial archives also preserved the recorded memory of the Ho past which can be invoked in reconstructing largely their pre-colonial history. See my essays 'Collective Memory and Reconstruction of Ho History', *Indian Folklore Research Journal*, Vol. 5, No.8, (December 2008), 87–103; 'Redefining Archaeology and the ethno-history of pre-colonial Singhbhum', presented at the International Seminar on *Applications of*

Anthropological Researches in Human Life organized by *The Asiatic Society*, (*Kolkata* on 7, 8, 9 January, 2009).

19. A.K. Sen, 'Conceptualization of the Hos of Singhbhum as a Tribe', in P.Sen (ed.), *Changing Tribal Life: A Socio-Philosophical Perspective*, Concept Publishing Company Pvt. Ltd., (New Delhi, 2003), pp. 1–12; 'Tribe-Peasant-Tribe Continuum: The Dynamics of Ho Identity', in S.Gopal (ed.), *Colonial India: A Centenary Tribute to Professor K.K.Datta*, Research Publication Series-4, Veer Kunwar Singh University, (Arrah, 2006), pp. 299–309.
20. Detection involved in historical research is suggested by Hayden White, *Tropics of Discourse: Essays in Cultural Criticism*, The Johns Hopkins University Press, (Baltimore and London, 1987), p. 84.
21. About the extension of an exotic culture in a tribal land see my 'Constructing a Different World: Pages from the Diary of Raisaheb Sashi Bhusan Sarkar', *Manwa Katha*, Vol. I, No. I., October 2007.
22. But that it still persists may be traced in some recent writings. In one such Ho participation in the Rebellion of 1857-58 has been attributed to feudal instigation and continuity of the historic linkages between the Ho and Arjun Singh, the raja of Porahat, in spite of the fact that the Ho had freed themselves from the control of local chiefs. Sanjukta Das Gupta, 'Rebellion in a Little Known District', pp. 110–11.
23. These are the broad traits of Ho culture the author has been able to glean from personal talks with Ho intelligentsia and social leaders. Such notions of community–identity seem to be intrinsic to *Adivasis* elsewhere. Hardiman notes that the *Adivasis* of Gujrat were united by a consciousness of common material circumstances and culture and a distance from non-*Adivasi* culture. They considered drinking and meat eating to be part of their identity while the Dangis affirmed their wildness through shifting cultivation and hunting. D. Hardiman, *The Coming of the Devi: The Adivasi Assertion in Western India*, OUP, (Delhi, 1987), pp. 81–2, 201; A.Skaria, *Hybrid Histories: Frontiers and Wildness in Western India*, OUP, (Delhi, 1999), pp. 66–7, 71.
24. For a critique of the idea of 'the tribe as a given and unproblematic' see Sanjukta Das Gupta, 'The Changing World of the Singhbhum Hos, 1820-1932', *The Indian Historical Review*, XXXIII, I, (January 2006), pp. 76-98.

2

Territory, People and Polity: Land and Early Settlements

The erstwhile district of Singhbhum constituted the southeastern part of the Chotanagpur division. Lying between 21° 59' 0"'and 22° 53' 0" north latitude and 85° 2' 0" and 86° 56' 0" east longitude,[1] containing an approximate area of 4503 square miles.[2] It was bounded by Midnapur on the east, Mayurbhanj, Keonjhar and Bonai states on the south and Gangpur state as well as Ranchi on the west and by Ranchi and Manbhum on the north. The district was a hilly and forested tract with stretches of level and fertile land mostly forming its central part[3] Kolhan, where the Ho predominantly inhabited, formed its southwestern part. This open undulating tract extended over an area measuring from sixty miles in length north and south, and from thirty-five to sixty in breadth.[4] An elevated plateau, it varied between 750 feet above sea level near Chaibasa, the headquarters of the district, to upwards of 1000 feet on the south. Its north and northeastern parts were for the greater part open and undulating, with low isolated rocks scattered over the area having hardly a trace of jungle. It comprised numerous prosperous and well-cultivated villages The southern part was flat open with rich cultivable soil and was also thickly populated and well cultivated. The southeastern portions were covered with jungle and partly with mass of hill ranges. The western and the southwestern portions were mountainous, thickly forested and sparsely inhabited.[5] Physical features of Singhbhum greatly influenced moral and material culture of people as shown elsewhere in this book.

Before British conquest the political and cultural areas of Singhbhum and Kolhan were fluid.[6] The areas dominated by the Ho

Fig. 2.1: A birds eye view of Saranda

tribe, then locally famous as Kol homeland, were conquered by the British and were administratively constituted into the Kolhan Government Estate in 1837. As suggested in the next chapter perhaps the new administrative unit did not contain the entire politico-cultural space of the Ho in Kolhan. This can be understood from the debate centering round the boundary and nomenclature of Singhbhum. Porahat rajas claimed that the name of Singhbhum was derived from the patronymic of the Singh dynasty of Porahat. The other idea was that Singhbhum was named after *Singbonga* or the Sungod, whom

Fig. 2.2: Toybo falls, Saranda

the Ho revered as the Creator of the Universe.[7] These two views lead us to the nature of demography and polity. The first suggested the place being ruled by non-tribal raj while the second related pervasive Ho influence over it.

The history of Singhbhum predated both the foundation of Porahat raj and Ho domination over it. Strangely this history remained unexplored by the British ethnographers like Tickell, Dalton and Risley.[8] We first come across an account of early history of Singhbhum in O'Malley. This sparse and brief account only relates that this area was the seat of paleolithic civilization. It came to form a part of the Gupta empire under Samudragupta (335-75 AD). Not politically alone the region was significant commercially also as it fell on the trade route leading to the ancient seaport of Tamralipta or Tamluk. Next historical evidence places Singhbhum within *raja* Sasanka's empire in the 7th century AD.[9] During medieval period it was never conquered by Muslim rulers. But about this period the Saraks, Bhuiyans, Hos, Bhumijs and others entered Singhbhum in search of a habitat and area of influence.

The Hos and Bhumijs considered the Saraks as the pioneer. They were the lay Jainas who entered the hills and jungles of Singhbhum from neighbouring Manbhum district.[10] It is believed that they had control over large tracts of Singhbhum during the 14th and 15th centuries AD. The remnants of copper mines and large number of *surmi-durmi* tanks as well as the surviving mango groves of Sarak-origin not only resurrected Sarak-day past but later proved to be a major factor in deciding *khuntkatti* rights of villagers.[11] Perhaps the next to enter were the Bhuiyans.[12] They brought large areas of Singhbhum under their control, though it is difficult to ascertain its nature and extent. Tickell considered them to be 'an inoffensive, simple race but rich in cattle and industrious cultivators.' On the other hand, Dalton profiled them as a strong political and military force on which the Singh dynasty of Porahat had to depend.[13]

The probable time of the foundation of Porahat raj was the first decade of the 13th century AD. The Singhs claimed an origin from the Rathor Rajputs of Mewar. But their political and military relations with the Bhuiyans and induction of Pauri *devi*, a Bhuiyan goddess, as the tutelary deity of the dynasty contend this claim. The Singh rulers claimed suzerainty over the whole of Singhbhum including the Ho territories. But as I shall show later this claim was unfounded. In 1620 AD, the Porahat raj was branched off and separate rulerships were founded at Seraikela and Kharsawan. Dhalbhum formed part of the Bengal *Jungle Mahals*. Proprietors of this tract styled themselves as the *rajas*. In 1833, the estate was transferred from Midnapur to Manbhum. But it was incorporated with Singhbhum in 1846.[14]

Gonds and Bhumijs were the others who peopled Singhbhum. But we have very inadequate information about their immigration and role. We only know that the former was the offshoot of the same tribe inhabiting the Central Provinces. About the latter[15], who formed their settlements in some of the *pirs* of south Singhbhum[16], were called *Matkum* or middle by the Ho.

The most momentous event was, however, the entry and expansion of the Kol or Ho into and across Singhbhum. Originating from the Munda stock of Chotanagpur plateau they began to immigrate in groups into Singhbhum since around the 10th century AD. The hesitant and sporadic migratory Ho are believed to have settled first in northern parts of Singhbhum. As the legend goes they helped the Marwari *Singhvansis* to found the Porahat raj. Later they defeated the Saraks and drove them out of Singhbhum. Next they dislodged the Bhuiyans from their preponderant position.[17]

It appears that the Ho maintained friendly relations with the Singh dynasty for a long time. On a mutual agreement the former vacated their settlements in the northern parts of Singhbhum and moved towards the southern parts.[18] From Village Papers we learn that it had taken place sometimes in the 17th century AD.[19] Occupying major parts of southern Singhbhum, they later emerged as a threat to the Singh rulers of Porahat, Seraikela and Kharsawan as well as the *raja* of Mayurbhanj. The Hos successfully quelled the attacks of the *rajas* of Chotanagpur and Singhbhum as well as the *mahapatar* of Bamanghatty (under the *raja* of Mayurbhanj) launched between 1770 and 1800 AD. For these successes in the battlefields the Hos came to be known as the *Larka* or fighting Kols. The *raja* of Porahat was forced to seek British help in 1820 to subjugate the *Larkas*. The Hos were defeated and brought under the control of the chiefs of Porahat, Seraikela, Kharsawan and Mayurbhanj in 1821. Smarting under the grievance of subjugation, the vanquished conducted predatory raids into the territories of the local chiefs and the British. This invited

British military intervention in 1836 and the final surrender of the Ho in 1837. The same year the Kolhan Government Estate (KGE) comprising 26 *pirs* of 622 villages was formed.[20]

TRIBE, TRIBALISM AND BRITISH RULE

Empire building presaged knowledge of the terrain and people to be ruled. But at the start of this epistemic intervention the British-administrator-ethnographers could collate a rather sparse and undependable information on pre-colonial Ho past. With this knowledge-bank they conceptualized the Ho and the region they inhabited. To them Singhbhum district, rather KGE, was virtually a frontier, the other of the civilized, a 'zone of anomaly'.[21] This otherness meant generally its intractable geographical locus due to forests and hills and other factors. But as I shall detail below this intractability was differential and not uniform.

The Ho ethnicity had distinct contents. It was first their affinity for a territory called Kolhan, their 'permanent home.' Second was their distinct language, rather a dialect, that marked the major differentia between the Munda and Ho.[22] But more significantly British ethnographers defined them as the linguistic buffer of the languages of Sanskrit-origin. To quote:

> 'Ethnologically their position is singular and interesting; speaking themselves the Kol language only they occupy a basin whose barrier of hills restrains the flow and blending together of the three great Sanskrit derivatives Hindi, Bengali and Uriya which but for this obstacle of an insulated language would have formed a trijunction boundary point in the centre of Singhbhum'.[23]

The community was found to represent a distinct polity. Roughsedge mentioned about unique Ho village administration through the Mundas and Mankis.[24] Dalton used Ho political system of 'confederate village communities under hereditary headmen' to distinguish them from the state system of local chiefs.[25] Having no 'evidence of stable polity' or 'locus of governance'[26], this pre-state system provided perhaps a possible logic for their incorporation into the British state system.[27]

The Ho as the other had other motifs. They were first ferocious and savage[28]; their setting was natural because they lived 'their own lives, free and unrestrained in the jungles or on the hills of Singhbhum'[29]; and last their nature was marked by simplicity, 'love for truth', 'honesty', and 'happy ingenuous disposition'. All these underlined them as natural compared to the people representing culture.[30] But significantly even the British found that this dichotomy was not uniform. Kolhan and the Ho were divided into zones of nature and culture. The Ho of northern Kolhan, locating many prosperous and well-cultivated villages, were more civilized compared to the wilder kinsmen of the south[31], which was an inaccessible forest hilly zone. About it a British official wrote—

> 'roads there were none, only jungal-paths from village to village. Now and again the forest was so thick that it was almost impossible for one man to walk along, and a way through had to be cut as they advanced. Range after range of hills had to be crossed where progress was slow and difficult.'[32]

Fig. 2.3: Impenetrable Saranda

We will see later that this was the locale to explain the shades in Ho militancy or Ho society being materially layered.[33]

Difference next took the form of inter-tribe otherness. The British focused on the distinction between the Ho and the Munda of the

Chotanagpur plateau first in 'manners, dialect, dress and appearance'[34] and then in the quality of their physique. Roughsedge observed that the Ho superiority in 'size and form' to their brethren in Chotanagpur was that of 'wild buffaloes to the village herds'.[35] Significantly however in British perception central difference was between the Ho and Hindu or rather Brahmanical Hinduism, suggested to be the mainstream of Hindustan.[36] It was pitched around distinct life styles and deportment[37], which Roughsedge, an early British general, reasoned as the principal cause of Ho hostility towards upper castes and also Muslims.[38]

Source. E.T. Dalton, Descriptive Ethnology

Fig. 2.4: A Ho in the 1870s

Thus the above cognitive project of colonial officials identified the Ho as culturally, ethnically and politically other. They believed that this identity had to be preserved as far as practicable from outside influence. But along with this colonial rulers thought that it was equally necessary to selectively inject doses of western modernity represented by the British to civilize the 'savage'. With this mindset the British mediation of Ho life began. This resulted in the slow and steady recreation of the tribe and their territory.

Formally incorporated into the British state system as part of the South West Frontier Agency (SWFA) in 1837 Kolhan was excluded from the operation of the general regulations[39] that governed other parts of India. Wilkinson founded an exclusive system of governance, which came to be called the Wilkinsonian system. This system was under the superintendence and direct control of the district head who was supposed to be the *ma-bap* of the simple Kolhan people. Civil and criminal rules were framed which administered justice with the help of village and *pir* heads. Though the Criminal Procedure Code was later implemented, the Civil Procedure Code was never introduced in Kolhan.[40]

The exotic system of land revenue survey and settlement was introduced for the first time in 1837. The first two settlements were *hal*[41] settlements[42] when an amount of eight anna per *hal*, increased to one rupee in 1854, was fixed as rent. In 1867, stick-measure was introduced and the rent was raised to two rupees. The feature of 1895 settlement was qualitative classification of land into *bera*, *bad* and *gora* with respective rate of rents.[43] Land revenue administration on the one hand progressively augmented the earning of colonial government from Rs. 5108 in 1837-38, to Rs. 8523 in 1852-53, to Rs. 64,828 in 1867, Rs. 1,77,300-1-3 in 1895 and Rs. 2,52,351 in 1918, and on the other extended the area of cultivation[44] from 3,35,735 acres during 1895-1897 to 4,33,334 acres during 1913-18.[45]

Exotism was entrenched further by colonial forest policy. Singhbhum, more so the KGE, abounded in primeval forests. The Saranda jungle is famous world over for its dense forest of *sal* trees. Reared in the midst of nature having close affinity with the adjacent natural forests, *Adivasis* in general claimed a natural right over the forests, numerous uses[46] of which had prompted them to identify their existence with nature around them. This notion of customary rights was encroached into when the British reserved 531 sq. mile and protected 212 sq. mile areas out of a total Kolhan land mass of 1954.91 square miles i.e. over a quarter of the total area.[47] Unhindered and free collection of forest products stopped. Firewoods, thatching grass, fodder grass, date palm, *sal* and other leaves, bamboo and other minor produce could be collected only on payment of an annual rate of two pice per rupee of land rent payable by them. People were allowed to cut green trees or timber only for private use. They could no longer graze their cattle, other than sheep or goat, in the reserved and protected areas.[48] This concept of forest rights was undoubtedly abominable for the Ho. Moreover, reserved forests at many places encroached into their supposed *khuntkatti* territory held sacrosanct by them. The presence of the *sasandiris* found within the reserved forests proved this point.[49] Popular protests against the forest policy by the Kolhan followed.[50]

The British introduced modern means of communication mainly to promote administration and commerce. Right from the beginning of colonial rule gravel and metal roads were constructed. By the 1910s in Singhbhum the total road-length under the maintenance by the Public Works Department was 47 miles and 452 ½ miles by the District Road Committee. This connected Chaibasa with Chakradharpur, Ranchi, Purulia, Bankura, Midnapur, Mayurbhanj and Keonjhar.[51] The isolation of Kolhan, including its villages, was somewhat removed and commerce was promoted. But the meagre and poor road network impeded development as exposed by an essay of this volume.[52]

More historic however was the introduction of the railways since the 1890s. It came to Singhbhum through the opening up of the Southeastern railways, which connected Howrah with Bombay. Through Chakradharpur, a distance of 25 kms. from Chaibasa, Kolhan was linked to other parts of the country. The Amda-Jamda rail lines were built to exploit the forest and mineral resources of Kolhan.[53] Though the railways served colonial policies, the passenger traffic as gathered from Ratneshvar's Tour Diary remained neglected.

When the Company government commenced the conquest of Kolhan, the British were not aware of the tremendous mineral resources of Kolhan. But in the 1850s, they could learn about the availability of copper and gold in Singhbhum. This inspired survey and prospecting by foreign companies. Since the 1920s, the rich reserve of iron ore, manganese, limestone etc. were discovered, which was followed by unprecedented mining activities in Kolhan and other parts of Singhbhum.[54] This opened an otherwise insulated Kolhan to outsiders, which is detailed later Mines provided jobs to the people. The *Adivasis* of Kolhan, particularly those with marginal landholdings, were found interested in part-time unskilled mining jobs to supplement family income. This additional job opportunity cannot however be specified[55] to assess its role in poverty alleviation

Introduction of market economy had been innovative for Kolhan. Pre-British economy was based on barter system with a limited commercial link with outside. As related elsewhere during colonial rule the number of *hats* not only increased but people also imbibed market-culture. Barter gradually yielded place to money economy. Exotic measures of *chatak,* seer, *paseri* and maund came into use. Not only forest but also agricultural products were marketed, causing a break in their tendency to produce for the family needs.[56] Market places grew to be the locus of intense economic activity where the people more so the *Adivasis* came into growing contact with *diku* traders. As actors in this competitive economic scene, both as a buyer and seller, a tribal slowly but steadily acquired individualistic and acquisitive traits.

Fig. 2.5: A village *hat*

Modern education entered Kolhan to combat witchcraft. The Anglo-Hindi school was opened at Chaibasa in 1841. But for lack of response it was closed down in 1851. Bengali-medium schools at Chaibasa, Cheri and Jayantgarh, founded later in Kolhan, suffered the same fate. A middle English school was next founded in 1865. It was followed by several primary and middle schools as well as *pathsalas* in Kolhan with the facility of teaching both English and Hindi. This was obviously in response to people's inclination for literate education, which is exemplified by almost village-wise figures of school-going children in the 1920s. Kolhan oral society was thus exposed to literate culture, exotic languages like English, Hindi, Bengali and Uriya and curriculum distinctly different from their indigenous mode of training and education. Literate Hos, a growing section in Ho society, emerged who had the capability to read, write and interpret the official orders and summons issued to their kinsmen or interact with the government on matters relating to Ho life.[57] But the corpus of Ho intelligentsia was frail. Different grades of schools in Singhbhum numbered 423 in 1908 out of which primary schools alone numbered 400. Zila School at Chaibasa was the only high school in the district.[58] Teaching perceptively suffered due to the non-availability of qualified teachers and patent want of resources.[59] Moreover, lack of acquaintance with the modern idea due to want of higher education[60] did not allow Ho intelligentsia to play the modernizer. Leadership remained predominantly in the hands of village-*pir* heads with whom the government preferred to interact to decide official policies regarding Kolhan indigenes.[61]

Decades of British rule changed Kolhan life. One major change was in the nature of demography. This was featured by the growing induction of outsiders, both ethnic and spatial, termed as *dikus* and a relative fall in the percentage of Ho population. In 1838-39 population of Kolhan was roughly estimated at 70,653, the ethnic break-up being 60,366 Hos i.e. about 85 per cent of the total and 10,287 non-Hos. The latter were the functional castes, the supposed offsprings of Aryan settlers. In 1867, the population stood at 1,18,281 of which 93,968 were Hos i.e. about 78 per cent, the rest being identified as Hindus.[62] It shows that after the consolidation of British rule outsiders steadily entered for government jobs, trade and commerce. Their number rose further by the turn of the century. The table below of 1891 census shows the ethnic division:

Aboriginal tribes	1,75,683	74.2%
Semi-Hinduized aboriginals	7,827	3.3%
Hindus	49,724	20.9%
Christians	2,106	0.9%
Mohammedans	1,441	0.6%
Unknown and Unspecified castes	449	0.1%

Source: Craven, *Final Report*, para 66.

This included both old *dikus*, i.e., those settled in Kolhan before 1867 and their children and new *dikus* or those who had immigrated after 1867. The demographic balance further tilted as we see the Census of 1911:

Animists	2,13,128
Hindus	80,798
Mohammedans	2,194
Christians	1,756

Source: Tuckey, *Final Report*, paras 18-20.

It meant that animists or aboriginals further came down to about 71 per cent of whom Hos numbered approximately 2,00,000 and the rest were Bhuiyans, Oraons, Santals and Gonds. Hindus included mainly Goalas, Tantis, Lohars and Kumhars. The upper castes registered negligible presence in Kolhan villages. The new immigrants were mainly from Gaya, Hazaribagh and Ranchi in Bihar, Manbhun, Bankura and Midnapur in Bengal, Cuttack and Baleswar in Orissa as well as the United Provinces.[63]

Diku immigration changed Kolhan scenario. During early decades they were allowed servile positions in villages as herdsmen, weavers, potters and blacksmiths.[64] Though this was not inverted, a trend was noticeable of some of them acquiring *Adivasi* lands on *thika*, some even purchasing tribal lands. This way their influence tended gradually to grow in Kolhan life.[65] This naturally became an irritant for Ho society. But the greater problem was of land alienation from *Adivasis* to the colonial government, companies and individuals mainly promoted by the administration.[66]

Socio-cultural impact was no less profound. The Hos of Kolhan were forced to accept *diku* religions and *kajis*. Interaction with Hinduism was more comprehensive and relevant. It was because of the presence of Hindu elements in Kolhan and the Hindu world with which the Ho land was more or less surrounded.[67] On the other hand, the influence of Christianity and Islam was marginal. Though the conversion of Hos to Islam cannot be related due to lack of data, Christian-conversion and Ho students visiting Christian missionary schools were areas of acculturation between Ho and Christianity. This conversion was not however as large as it occurred elsewhere in Chotanagpur. Even then those who were converted were deprived of family property, as they could not perform the *jangtopa* or the last rites.[68] About *diku kajis* initial Ho allergy[69] gradually dissipated. This is borne out by younger generation's growing softness to non-Ho languages[70] and increasing presence of Ho children in schools. Ho preference for Hindi was however more noticeable, which prompted British officials to make it the official language in Kolhan.[71]

The impact of colonial rule on Ho culture was subversive. As we reach the turn of 19th and beginning of the 20th century we find a Kolhan perceptively different from pre-British Kolhan. The Ho 'village republics' had been incorporated into the British legal and administrative network with the Deputy Commissioner at the apex and Mankis and Mundas as the ground functionaries. This created a facade of a rule through the social leaders. It also created a strange duality in Ho life where he/she was culturally fastened to the community and *killi* but legally he/she was identified as an individual. This identification of a Ho as fostered by the land registrations promoted material and aggressive traits. This encouraged him/her to challenge indigenous institutions like lineage, *killi,* indigenous leaders and customs. The spate of court cases between a Ho and Ho, a family and family, *killi* and *killi* or a village and village not only showed heterogeneity but growing loss of faith in the Manki-Mundas and *panchs*.[72]

Colonial forest policy excluded a large forest area from Ho colonization, which in pre-British or even early decades of British rule was open to their expansion. The impact of this exclusion was profound. The Hos were confined to reclaimed or unreclaimed forest area within village boundary. This forced marginal landholders to migrate to neighbouring Keonjhar and Mayurbhanj for arable land or inflate the village labour force.[73] Next with growing pressure of population on land litigation for existing family lands increased. I am inspired to hazard the guess that when forest tract was easily available to colonize people preferred to move out than to fight among themselves.[74] This changed terrain and people broadly providing the backdrop. I now initiate the discussion on the state of current Ho historiography, which may inspire looking beyond the present corpus of knowledge.

NOTES

1. W.W. Hunter, *A Statistical Account of Bengal*, (*SAB*) Vol. XVII, Concept Publishing Company Pvt. Ltd., (Delhi, 1976), (1877), p. 17 Interestingly, the geographical position differs e.g. it is between 21° 30' and 23° north latitude and 85° and 86° east latitude in Tickell 'Memoir', p. 699 and

between 21° 58' and 22° 54' north latitude and 85° 0' and 86° 54' east longitude in O'Malley, *Bengal District Gazetteers,* p. 1.

2. Hunter, *SAB*, p. 1; Dalton, *Tribal History*, p. 177. But O'Malley found the district to measure 3891 square miles. *Bengal District Gazetteers*, p. 1.
3. O' Malley, *Bengal District Gazetteers*, pp. 1-2. In 1877 primeval forest covered about the two-third of the district. Hunter, *SAB*, p. 23.
4. Tickell, 'Memoir', p. 699.
5. Craven, *Final Report*, p. 2.
6. See Generalizations.
7. F.B. Bradley-Birt, *Chota Nagpor: A Little Known Province of the Empire*, (London, 1903), p. 82; H. Ricketts, *Report on the District of Singhbhoom vide Selections from the Records of Bengal*, No. XVI, (Calcutta, 1854), p. 69.
8. Tickell, 'Memoir'; Dalton, *Tribal History*; H.H.Risley, *The Tribes and Castes of Bengal*, Vol. 1, Firma Mukhopadhyay, (Calcutta, 1981), (1891). I have suggested the strategy to retrieve it and identified the broad areas that should be historicized in 'Redefining Archaeology and the ethno-history of pre-colonial Singhbhum'.
9. O'Malley, *Bengal District Gazetteers,* pp. 22–3.
10. Tuckey, *Final Report*, p. 18; Sahu, *The Kolhan*, pp. 8–9.
11. TSKP offer several such evidences of Sarak-presence which often challenged *khuntkatti* claims by the Hos.
12. Their racial origin however continues to be a debatable issue. The Bhuiyan chiefs considered themselves to be the Rajputs. But Dalton contended that they were of Dravidian stock.
13. Tickell, 'Memoir', pp. 696–7; Bradley-Birt, *Chota Nagpur*, p. 84; Dalton, *Tribal History*, p. 140.
14. Dalton, *Tribal History*, pp. 140, 179; P.C. Roychoudhury, *1857 in Bihar* (*Chotanagpur and Santhal Parganas*), (Patna, 1959), (1957), p. 71; Sahu, *The Kolhan*, p. 9. For a detailed history of the princely states of Seraikela and Kharsawan see C.K. Paty, 'History of Seraikela and Kharsawan States (1620-1956 A.D.)', Classical Publishing Company, (New Delhi, 2002), Chap. 2; Hunter, *SAB*, pp. 89–90. For the origin of Dhal *rajas* see Dalton, *Tribal History*, p. 176.
15. The Bhumijs had no traditions of their origin. The term meant 'the children of the soil'.
16. Dalton, *Tribal History*, pp. 173, 277; Tuckey, *Final Report.*, pp. 17–8; Bradley-Birt, *Chota Nagpur*, p. 85.
17. Tuckey, *Final Report*, p. 17; Bradley-Birt, *Chota Nagpur*, p. 85; Tickell, 'Memoir', p. 697. With the help of Village Papers I have made seminal attempt to reconstruct this phase. 'Collective Memory and Reconstruction of Ho History'.
18. Tickell, 'Memoir', pp. 696–7.
19. See TSKP.

20. Dalton, *Tribal History*, p. 180; Tickell, 'Memoir', p. 698; Singh, *The Ho Tribe*, Chap. III; Sahu, *The Kolhan*, p. 71.
21. For an elaboration of the notion of frontier and zone of anomaly. *see* A. Skaria, *Hybrid Histories: Forests, Frontiers and Wildness in Western India*, OUP, (Delhi, 1999), pp. 157–63; Sivaramakrishnan, *Modern Forests*, p. 39.
22. A.K.Sen, 'Conceptualization of the Hos of Singhbhum as a Tribe', in P.Sen (ed.), *Changing Tribal Life: A Socio-Philosophical Perspective*, Concept Publishing Company Pvt. Ltd., (New Delhi, 2003) pp. 1–14.
23. Dalton, *Tribal History*, p. 179.
24. See Generalizations for reference.
25. Dalton, *Tribal History*, pp. 178–80.
26. Sivaramakrishnan, *Modern Forests*, p. 36.
27. This was a motivating factor for Wilkinson. Sahu, *The Kolhan*, p. 71.
28. See Generalizations and Roughsedge's equation.
29. Bradley-Birt, *Chota Nagpur*, p. 85.
30. Tickell, 'Memoir', p. 706. Little commerce, allergy to money and poor agriculture were other suggested marks of naturality. Ibid., pp. 805–6.
31. Bradley-Birt, *Chota Nagpur*, pp. 88–9, 91. *See* next Chapter.
32. Bradley-Birt, *Chota Nagpur*, p. 91.
33. Further details in Generalizations and Social Stratification.
34. Tickell, 'Memoir', p. 803.
35. Dalton, *Tribal History*, pp. 180–81. One can presume that the like of Roughsedge and Tickell anticipated the ethnological approach that generally occupied the centrestage of British representation of the indigenes. For an incisive and detailed study though in a different context see Sangeeta Dasgupta, "From 'Description' to 'Definition': Mapping the Oraons and the 'tribe' in Chotanagpur", presented at St. Antony's College, (Oxford, May 2007).
36. In fact, for differences in religion, customs, appearance and language, the British considered the entire Jharkhand region to be an area out of the pale of Hindusathan. Ibid., p. 164.
37. Tickell maintained that Ho villages were free from disease as compared to other villages and from 'the vile traits of common Hindoostanee life'. Tickell, 'Memoir', pp. 706, 788, 803; Dalton, *Tribal History*, pp. 184–5.
38. See Roughsedge's equation.
39. The formation of the non-regulation system of the SWFA has been detailed in J.C. Jha, *The Tribal Revolt of Chotanagpur (1831-32)*, K.P. Jayaswal Research Institute, (Patna, 1987), pp. 241–5. About the politics of its constitution see Sivaramakrisnan, *Modern Forests*, p. 65.
40. A.K. Sen (ed.), *Wilkinson's Rules: Context, Content and Ramifications*, (Chaibasa, 1999), pp. XV-XVI, 17–21, 98–9.
41. The system of fixing rent on the basis of ploughs in use for cultivation.
42. In another tribal region land tax was fixed on the basis of *hal* or sickle. Hardiman, *The Coming of the Devi*, pp. 70–1.

43. This principle was somewhat akin to division of arable land in Chotanagpur into *don* or low lying land on which rice was cultivated and *tanr* or upland which grew millets, pulses and oilseeds. These two were further divided into three classes according to their level of productivity. Mohapatra, 'Class Conflict and Agrarian regimes', pp. 2–3.
44. This is instanced in a different tribal setting. Sivaramakrishnan, *Modern Forests*, pp. 46–7.
45. Details have been culled from Ricketts, *Report*, p. 70; Tuckey, *Final Report*, p. 2; Sahu, *The Kolhan*, pp. 152–7. In 1867 qualitative classification was introduced for the first time but only first two were assessed.
46. This symbiotic relationship was typical of Indian tribes. For another instance see J.Reid, *Final Report on the Survey and Settlement Operations in the District of Ranchi, 1902-1910*, Bengal Secretariat Book Depot, (Calcutta, 1912), p. 126.
47. During 1913-18 the reserved area increased to 537 sq. miles and protected area came to 1,919 sq. miles. Tuckey, *Final Report*, p. 2.
48. Craven, *Final Report*, pp. 32–3, 36.
49. T.S. McPherson, *Final Report on the Operations for the Preparation of a Record of Rights in Pargana Porahat, District Singhbhum 1905-1907*, (Calcutta, 1908), pp. 152–5. TSKP of Manoharpur *thana* area further show the forced migration from their villages due to colonial forest policy.
50. This finds an expression in Singhbhum 1927-30. For the policy and indigenous resistance in the context of Chotanagpur and Singhbhum see Damodaran, 'Indigenous Forests', pp. 115–50; A.K. Sen,'Protected Forest Rules and Ho Social Protest', vide C.K. Paty (ed.), *Forest, Government and Tribe*, Concept Publishing Company Pvt. Ltd., (New Delhi, 2006), pp. 78–88.
51. Moreover 127 miles of village tracts were maintained by the funds of the KGE, O'Malley, *Bengal District Gazetteers*, pp. 160–61.
52. See Singhbhum 1927-30.
53. O'Malley, *Bengal District Gazetteers*, p. 160; P.C. Roychoudhury, *Bihar District Gazetteers Singhbhum*, (Patna, 1958), pp. 205–6. The areas of the rail-routes formed the mineral-forest-rich zones of Kolhan.
54. O'Malley, *Bengal District Gazetteers*, pp. 140–51.
55. We can however form a rough idea of the quantum of labour employment provided in the last chapter.
56. See Generalizations and Roughsedge's equation.Tickell, 'Memoir', p. 805; Craven, *Final Report*, p. 14. For items of export see Craven, *Final Report*, p. 15 and earlier trend see Tickell,'Memoir', p. 805.
57. O'Malley, *Bengal District Gazetteers*, pp. 201–5; Tuckey Settlement Village Notes. Here I have in mind the *gitiora* mode of training where children were taught the dos and donts of life. Lists of Permanent Establishment of the Deputy Commissioner, Singhbhum available at the District Record Room, Chaibasa inform us about Ho gentlemen working at local offices. They also include some of the Mankis and Mundas. Local administration introduced literacy criterion for appointment to these offices.

58. O'Malley, *Bengal District Gazetteers*, p. 202.
59. This conclusion becomes inevitable from a reading of the annual educational reports contained in the Land Revenue Administration Reports.
60. There was no college in Kolhan during British rule.
61. Craven and Tuckey Settlement Village Papers show that the village and *pir* heads were generally consulted in the solution of inter-village disputes or those relating to Ho customs
62. Dalton, *Tribal History*, p. 185; Col. E. T. Dalton, Commissioner of Chotanagpore to T.B. Lane, Secretary to the Board of Revenue, Lower Provinces, No. 754, 6 April 1867, Revenue Department, June 1867, Proceeding No. 122, p. 128.
63. One gets the impression from village-wise population figuers in the Village Notes. In 1881 Brahmins numbered 98 and Rajputs 82, Craven, *Final Report*, Appendix A, p. IV; O'Malley, *Bengal District Gazetteers*, p. 48.
64. Hunter, *SAB*, p. 36.
65. Details are provided in village-wise *thika* list in Craven and Tuckey Settlement Village Papers or *Diku* Reports.
66. We get an idea from Singhbhum 1927-30.
67. Hindu-Ho interaction is detailed in the next Chapter.
68. This problem is met in Craven Settlement Village Papers and TSKP. I study this in 'From Village Elders to British Judge'.
69. I have in mind Ho sensitivity towards their own *kaji* related elsewhere and failure of early Bengali, English and Hindi-medium schools due to Ho mal-adjustment with them.
70. Dalton, *Tribal History*, p. 185.
71. Hunter, *SAB*, pp. 36-7.
72. Craven Settlement Village Papers on disputes or Tuckey Settlement *Tanaza* papers, U/S 83 and TSKP.
73. Hundreds of Hos, mainly living in south Kolhan, migrated to adjacent Mayubhanj and Keonjhar states where they were offered rent-free lands for cultivation and where they could use the forests more freely than they could in Kolhan. LRAR 1907-8, DC's Office, GD, RB, CN XI Returns, FN 16, para 21
74. This was socially enjoined and sanctioned. S.J. Manook, the Assistant Commissioner of Singhbhum informed 'If there are two *khets* (Italics mine) and three sons, the third son must shift for himself. It often happens that if the holding of the father is small, the brother makes it all over to the eldest, and the others try to do what they can, but still their claim exists and is never destroyed.' S.J. Manook to C.H. Bompas, Deputy Commissioner of Singhbhum, 3 September 1895 appended to J.A. Craven to the Deputy Commissioner, No. 108 dated 21 August, 1895 vide W.H. Grimley to the Secretary to the Board of Revenue, Lower Provinces, No. 876LR, 14 October, 1895, Revenue Department, File No.16-S/2 Nos. 113-4. This relates to the Settlement of Kolhan Government Estate in Singhbhum.

3

Generalizations, Confusions and Reconstruction of Ho Historiography

This chapter examines the available corpus of Ho history. As related before the archival sources of select places more or less provided the basic material on which this corpus had been constructed. Knowledge-making being an integral part of colonial system of governance it largely foregrounded administratively useful information. But even with this basic flaw colonial data generally marked the beginning of recorded knowledge about the Ho rather tribal past.

This was mainly because pre-literate Ho society had the tradition of conserving their past in the memories of their elders. But the sense of both space and time was peculiar to them. They knew the meaning of a village and possibly a bigger unit called *pir*.[1] They were aware of the time of festivals and agricultural seasons. Family and village genealogies were what they could retain somewhat definitely punctuated by a major event that had affected their collective life. These events could be origin of a village, names of Manki and Munda being linked with the first entry of a family or *killi* into the village, the upheaval like the revolt of 1857 and the names of such major players as Tickan Saheb (Tickell) or Arjun Singh.[2] But the collective recall happened largely to be rather hesitant and laboured. Songs and legends of Ho pre-British past did not survive, even if these had ever formed part of their oral tradition.[3] So history of the Hos of Singhbhum is more or less the British-recorded history. This British historical tradition is temporally precise and factually more elaborate.

However, on a critical reading of the data it becomes clear to a scholar, having greater access to district-level papers, that the existing Ho historiography rests on certain dominant categories, which were often drawn on the basis of hasty and misconceived generalizations from facts culled from the official documents of the British period. Unfortunately, this colonial legacy continued to influence Ho studies long into British rule.

Divided into three broad sections, this chapter first takes up the mechanism of forming judgments on a reading of the situation; it then seeks to identify some of the major generalizations to internally critique these with the help of archival evidences. In a sense these two sections broadly examines the text, i.e. the existing historical corpus of Singhbhum and Ho. The third begins the quest of going beyond by seeking to prepare kind of a blueprint on which a reconstruction may begin.

GENERALIZING MODALITY

While drawing generalizations on the basis of available sources British ethnographers did an historical act, as this constitutes both the means and goal of history.[4] Again when this was invoked as an explaining tool they rightly crafted history. But a researcher should be skeptical to all those inferences which were not logically drawn. Knowing that in inductive methods conclusions remain probable[5], inferences are scientific and their truth-probability becomes much greater when supportable evidences are more numerous, objectively collated and analyzed. When we examine the generalizations drawn by British ethnographers about Singhbhum and Ho we find that these were based often on inadequate data.[6] Moreover, conclusions were drawn ignoring contrary evidences due to ideological angularity of chroniclers. As a result these conceptualizations tended to be both hasty and undependable. These dominant but doubtful historical categories need to be questioned if we seek to reconstruct Ho past.

THE CONCEPT OF HO LAND: HODESUM VS KOLHAN

According to British administrative ideology in order to be known as a homogenous group the people must have a territory of its own. But in respect of the Ho early British ethnographers faced a baffling problem. Though a certain tract with a predominantly Ho population[7] was named the Kolhan Government Estate they found that as a geographical and political unit Kolhan had been a nebulous idea. It is understood to be the variant of the Sanskrit root 'Kolsthan', i.e. land of the Kols.[8] But it is doubtful whether the British were familiar with the exact etymological origin of the word. What they seemed to reason was the preponderance of Kols in the given area. Now let us try to delineate what this area was.

It is a fact that historically the Hos were not confined to a fixed territory. When groups of Mundas migrated into Singhbhum, they first located themselves in 'the open tract now called Singhbhoom and the Kolehan.'[9] This tract was then under the Bhuiyans who allowed the immigrants to 'form settlements in the neighbouring woods' and reside in the central open tracts. Perhaps here these communities lived either together or side by side. But this Bhuiyan or Ho-dominated spaces cannot be exactly delineated from the available evidences. We then learn that at a later unspecified time, a fight ensued between the Saraks, the lay Jainas inhabiting parts of Singhbhum, and Hos. Finally, the latter expelled the former from the area, which Tickell identified as 'Kolehan'. But again this tract cannot be delineated nor can we say if it was called Kolhan then. It seems probable that after this success fresh waves of Ho immigration increased their number in their area of control. This numerical strength and political power understandably converted the place into a Kol territory. But later they did not remain confined to that space also. After helping the 'Rajputs' from Marwar[10] to defeat the Bhuiyans, the Hos entered into a political alliance with the Rajputs. With this help the Singhs 'established themselves in Porahaut and the rich open plains to the northward' and the Hos 'withdrew to the remaining tract of open land'. But this unspecified[11] open land did not confine total Kol space for long. They soon spread southwards and colonized major parts of southern Singhbhum. Perhaps due to this Kol hegemony, the area came to be locally known as Kol territory during pre-colonial period. As stated before in 1837 the British conquered this area and named it the Kolhan Government Estate.

During later British period changing number of Kolhan villages confounds the confusion further. We learn that the number rose from 622 in 1837 to 786 in 1855 and then to 847 in 1867.[12] Here I would like to focus on the numerical enigma. Though both Craven and Tuckey Settlement papers indicate the setting up of new villages due to rise in population out of mother villages, a sharp rise from 622 to 786 between 1837 and 1855 seems somewhat intriguing. The rise in population in less than two decades could never have been so great as to cause the birth of 164 new villages within that short span. In fact instead of a rise, population registered a fall from 70,653 in

1838-39 to 68,301 in 1854.[13] In this context it may be proposed that what the British conquered in 1837 was only that area comprising 622 villages, which was once under the chiefs of Porahat, Seraikela, Kharsawan and Mayurbhanj. It may just be that a sizeable number of these 164 villages represented that part of later British-day Kolhan, which was outside any control, perhaps true and unaffected Kol land. One would perhaps appropriate exact name and area of these villages if he/she were able to compare the list of villages mentioned by Tickell in his letter to his superior[14] with the list of villages in Craven and Tuckey Settlement Reports. Besides solving the problem of exact Kolhan territoriality, it might also tell us about the more original Ho and their way of life. Perhaps this might also solve the riddle of the exact extent of Porahat *rajas* control which the existence of *raja*-controlled pockets as Jagannathpur and Jaintgarh in predominant Ho territory of south Kolhan raises in our mind. We may also collate information about the time and occasion of the end of *raja's* predominance there as well as subsequent Ho expansion into that region.

Temporality and territoriality are not the only confusions emerging from extant historical sources. British-day ethnographers debated whether the Ho homeland should be called Kolhan or Hodesum. The debate seemed to be inaugurated by Tickell when in 1840 he wrote 'Memoir on the Hodesum (improperly called Kolehan)'. The author appears to be the most anthropologically precise among early British officials. He understood the generic expression of Kol, Munda as its species and then the distinction between Munda and Ho.[15] Interestingly his predecessors in Singhbhum were not so informed. E. Roughsedge used the expression 'Cole'.[16] For him therefore the land was Kolhan. T. Wilkinson, the first political agent of the South West Frontier Agency, was equally imprecise when he framed his rules in 1837 for the administration of criminal and civil justice for Kolhan and Bamanghatty.

Obviously, the ground knowledge of Tickell, who served as the first administrative head of the district between May 1837 and May 1840, was much greater.[17] He was enjoined by Wilkinson, his superior in office, to be kind of *ma bap* for the people he was supposed to administer.[18] A perusal of his 'Memoir' reveals that local informants and his field knowledge largely provided him the database. He was aware of the Kolarian people inhabiting Chotanagpur plateau. But he also knew the distinction between the parent Munda stock and its progeny the Hos. Tickell wrote:

> 'They (Hos) have separated themselves entirely from the race from which they sprang viz. the Moondas of Eastern Chootia Nagpoor ...When the separation took place, it is impossible to say but it has become marked not only in manners, dialect and dress, but in appearance.'[19]

So according to Tickell the evolution of Honess among erstwhile Mundas was complete, at least at the point of his engagement, causing not only spatial severance of the break-away group but fructification of distinct Ho identity also. This manifested in the growing number of exclusive Ho *killi*s as well as the origin of the Ho dialect. On this basis Tickell preferred the term Hodesum in place of Kolhan.

From Tickell the cue passed to Hayes. He reported that the Kols of Singhbhum called themselves Hos and their country the Hodesum.[20] But after him British chroniclers showed their clear preference for the term Kolhan instead of Hodesum. Even with the knowledge of distinct Ho ethnicity Dalton named the Ho land as Kolhan.[21] The same expression was used by Craven and Tuckey also.[22] Though British officials were conscious of the demographic difference between different groups of Kolarian people[23], in the context of Kolhan, such expressions as Kol and Ho were used in general as synonyms. This semantic dilution deprives us of the opportunity of addressing the processes of gradual growth of Honess, of birth of non-Munda *killi*s and evolution of exogamic and endogamic norms of marriage among Hos. These crucial aspects of Ho history may form themes of further research.

HO OR KOL AS *LARKA*

During British rule the Kols or Hos had been generally termed as *Larka* or fighting Kols. In 1820 when the British army was involved in a military encounter with the tribals of Singhbhum we find frequent use of *Larka* Cole or simply *Larka* or Cole. But even after that when only *Larka* or Cole was used, it also implied the suffix of Cole or prefix of *Larka*.[24] Tickell set the trend of using *Larka* Kol with the synonym of Ho[25], which Hayes, Dalton and Craven[26] later followed. Since then the use of *Larka* prefix became less frequent and that of simply Kol or Ho more common.[27]

This semantic choice was visibly influenced by immediate experience of Ho militancy against the British during 1819-20. This was reinforced by locally adduced information of Kols successfully resisting local chiefs to conquer them in near past.[28] After a few years Tickell collected the folklore that the dreaded community of Kols had worsted Saraks at an unidentified past.[29] This seemed to impact the categorizing of the Kols as *Larka* Kol by British ethnographers also. But it creates a problematic. Early British representation generally undermined the saga of Kol bravery and love for freedom. Instead it created the impression that they were essentially predatory, aggrandizing and bloodthirsty group of people with no civilized feature in them. Such expressions as 'wild', 'savage' and a 'dreadful pest to the civilized part of Singhbhum' are very common. [30] In fact to the British this savagery was animalish though this conclusion was drawn even when contrary evidences of a civilized life were there.[31] What is intriguing is that this image of the Ho premised the subsequent formulation of British tribal policy in Singhbhum as elaborated in a subsequent chapter.

Next point I want to make is that Ho *larkaness* was not uniform but somewhat layered impacted as it was by differential material development. The areas of northern Kolhan where Ho settlements were older and people were more developed; they were less *larka* than those of less advanced areas of southern Kolhan. Moreover, pervasive militancy which Roughsedge came across in 1819-20 did not endure for long. After initial resistance many heads of Ho villages submitted to the *raja* of Porahat. Similarly, some Mundas and villages submitted after initial fight and helped the British army against their 'brethren in arms.'[32] This fissure in Kol ranks widened later. When Wilkinson began his offensive against *Larka* Kols in 1836-37, the story of a section of Kols surrendering after initial fight and another showing much greater valour and resistance was replicated. But the greater reality was that people helped the British against their own men. The division of Ho community into friendly and refractory Kols diluted the monolithic notion of *Larka*.[33]

The sweeping objectification of the tribe as *Larka* Kol therefore raises many questions. The first is that if the entire community were uniformly war mongering why its mental attitude was not generally aggressive and hawkish? Instead what we find is the quiet and peaceful rhythm of Ho village life, a healthy balance between sexes, docile rather henpecked image of the husband[34] and more so the absence of any *larka* cult in their pantheon. Secondly, did the Larka-savage fixation not cause the neglect of the study of evolving Ho culture in early, as also. Later ethnography? This was why the like of Tickell, Dalton, Craven and Tuckey produced more or less sketchy and synchronic accounts which whetted our appetite but failed to satiate it. Thirdly, we inherit an inflated image of Ho savagery and brutality, which extended into post-independence historiography. This causes a neglect of peace-day situation, the normal flow of their familial and village life, relationship between a husband and wife, children and parents, their political and social institutions and various changes taking place in their world-view. Perhaps the time has come for us to appropriate this normal flow of life, for subaltern history is to be gleaned more from daily chores of the hut and not the booths from which they fought their battles. This will be possible if we are able to extricate Ho studies from its *Larka* fixation, not however shifting our attention from the recrudescence of extraordinary courage and bravery by the Hos.[35] We have a clue from the British recorded history itself to programme this parallel representation. This clue is provided by Tickell who observed that predatory raids of *Larkas* 'were never marked by cruelty or unnecessary violence, nor except when they were openly resisted, was ever life taken.'[36] This will perhaps make us understand that peace and quiet was natural of Ho life; bow and arrow were wielded only when they feared that the normal rhythm of their mundane life might be aggressed by an external element.

THE NOTION OF INSULATION

The insulation of Kolhan from other parts of the country and of the Ho from other communities is the dominant projection of the land and the people. Of the three types of insulation highlighted by British ethnographers first was geographical. It was remarked that nature had designed hill and jungle-clad Singhbhum for the Ho[37], to reason their difference from outside world and people. Next was the notion of exclusive Ho political space, an idea that seemed to have originated after the Ho defeated Saraks. Due to the prevailing fear about them the pilgrims to Puri desisted from settling there.[38] It implied that Ho political sensitivity had developed so much around a certain tract that they considered this to be their exclusive domain. We have further support from Dalton. He informed that even thirty-five years after the formation of the Kolhan Government Estate old Hos considered Kolhan as 'an exclusive Ho territory' and did not allow aliens to hold lands near their villages.[39]

The third but more dominant and continuous criterion was that of ethno-cultural exclusiveness. Roughsedge was the father of this idea. He wrote:

> 'Not having any of the feelings of veneration for Bramins, cows which pervade Hindoos of every description they make no scruple of putting to death any man of respectable caste who presumed to enter their territory, nor is there I can venture to affirm a single Bramin, Rajpoot or Mussulman in any one of the numerous and well inhabited villages they possess.' [40]

This affirmed that the Hos nurtured a strong physical hostility towards Hindus, rather upper castes and Muslims. Though the notion of physical hostility was later mellowed, Roughsedge's, paradigm had its echo in later official accounts also. While Tickell formulated the difference between Hos and Hindus[41], writing about 'jealous isolation' of Hos Dalton emphasised their contempt for 'all other classes' more so the Hindus.[42] Even as late as 1920 Tuckey reported that Hos had maintained their exclusiveness to a large extent and they refused to have any intercourse with 'Dikkus.'[43]

This notion of Ho isolation seemed to lay in the logic of history. We know that the Kolarian main stock suffered prolonged trauma of displacement and migration, which ultimately led them into Chotanagpur plateau.[44] But from there also a section of the Mundas had to migrate into Singhbhum, where after long years of tribulation and uncertainty they could entrench themselves.[45] Consequently, they became very sensitive towards their homeland, inspiring them to live in isolation from others.

However, notion of isolation has been exaggerated. We know that figuring insulation was a colonial strategy to facilitate infiltration of western ideas and institutions among subject people. On the basis of archeological findings it has been shown that though contrasts had existed between 'the civilized and their domesticated landscape and the savages in their wild woods', 'the boundaries and aspirations of communities were defined by the presence of other communities, other ways of living.'[46] Similarly, an anthropologist also maintained that contact between tribal people of India and cattle-rearing people living in the more open plains had been continuous.[47] We have strong evidence from our own area of study to substantiate that neither both Kolhan and the Ho were totally insulated nor these people were both mentally and physically allergic to outside influence and outsiders.

I shall first cull evidence from Roughsedge. He reported that about fifty years ago Porahat *rajas* held some control over the *Larkas*.[48] Though this control was weakened later, a political link continued between them and local chiefs. This was the precise reason why they sided with the latter in their military squabbles.[49] But this was not the only area of the inclusiveness of Kolhan tribesmen. They had material link with non-Hos perhaps right from the beginning of their settled life. To quote Roughsedge:

> 'They allow to reside in villages under great subjection, a few *pahuns* (weavers), *gwallas*, and *conchus* (potters) for the sake of being provided with cloth, pots and *ghee* (the former generally act as interpreters and accountants when occasion requires).'[50]

The last bracketed information had the portent of non-tribals playing as an intermediary between a Kolhan Ho and an outsider. Moreover, we learn that the Ho travelled all the way to Puri for salt and that cocoons reared by them were bartered to itinerant bead merchants in return for necklaces.[51] These indicate that these people had commercial intercourse with outside world.

The contact was wider resulting in Hindu neighbours exercising moral influence over the Ho. Tickell admitted:

> 'The Hos, although totally distinct from Hindoos yet, being a simple race have suffered that crafty people to lure them in many ways into following their ceremonies, rites, festivals, and prejudices. Those near the boundaries have become as subservient to Brahmins as any Hindoos would be.'[52]

The depth of this moral influence can be understood if we decode Ho origin myth. They believed that they were created together with Bhumijs, Bhuiyans, Santals as well as Brahmins, Rajputs, Chattris and others.[53] This showed that the Hos had a mental space for non-tribals, rather caste Hindus also. This seemed to grow with years when the younger generation became more receptive to non-tribal languages and the community allowed new settlements of Goalas, Kurmis and others in Kolhan.[54]

This ambivalent situation put the British rulers in a great fix. They had both to segregate the tribe from outsiders and yet encourage *diku* influx to serve their imperial institutions and material interests. For these Kolhan had increasingly more to be opened paving the way for the entry of non-ethnic outsiders. This stepped up the process of their infiltration to such an extent that Kolhan had hardly a few villages with exclusive Ho population.[55] This gradually broadened the area of contact further. Indigence and lure of material progress gradually intensified the process of Ho migration to Keonjhar and Mayurbhanj for cultivable lands and to Assam for tea garden jobs.[56]

Subsequently, the cultural hiatus between Hos and others decreased further. After the opening up of the Churches some Hos went to the fold of Christianity.[57] Ho parents sent their children to Christian missionary schools.[58] The Hindu influence was perhaps more pervasive. Village Papers bear testimony to Hos worshipping *Shiva*.[59] Over a much larger area we notice Goddess *Pauri* being worshipped along with village *Desauli*.[60] This reality was officially acknowledged:

> 'the general tendency of education is to make the Ho an agnostic or lean towards Hinduism...Had Hinduism been a proselytizing religion and had it admitted converts from other religions, it is probable a good many Hos would have gone to its fold.'[61]

In a recent study Areeparampil showed that this influence continued even later.[62] These evidences will inform a perceptive observer about the epistemic unsoundness of insulation and will perhaps apprise him of a historical situation being disproportionately presented to serve the imperialist purpose of divide and rule. But at the same time the above official observation should not carry us away. In a recent study on Hindu-*Adivasi* relations on a wider canvas it has rightly been shown that *Adivasis* including the Hos of Kolhan were not overwhelmed by the influence. The acculturation was both differential and selective.[63] The discussion continues in the next section.

THE CONCEPT OF *DIKU*

Insulation was the logic on which the concept of *diku* was grounded. Spelled variously as *diku*, *dikku* or *deko* the term has been defined in linguistic surveys, dictionaries, gazetteers to mean non-tribal out-groups with an emphasis on Hindus and having an oppressive connotation.[64] But particularly in the context of Kolhan one would be struck by the nebulosity of meaning and failure of the British to precisely define the term. This failure may be attributed to paucity of information and the logic of British imperialism. Appropriation of information in Kolhan was influenced by the depth and extent of control of the colonizer over the colonized. Early British ethnographers lacked precise knowledge about non-Hos living in Kolhan.[65] But during Tuckey Settlement they found that several Kolhan villages were founded by non-Hos. While this epistemic change is understandable, what seems intriguing is that knowledge-quest was need-specific. So efforts to acquire more data on ethnic outsiders grew with the gradual intensification of the problem of *diku*. Here epistemology had been used as a tool of colonialism.[66] A student of Ho studies must understand this historical position before accepting this demographic difference as essential.

In defining Ho otherness British ethnographers used different criteria. They began with an ethnic difference between a Ho and Hindu. Here confusion seemed to prevail among British officials whether this Hindu belonged to higher or lower caste. As stated before Roughsedge emphasized Ho hostility towards upper caste men as they allowed functional castes to reside in their villages. Seemingly in early ethnography a *diku* was an upper caste. Dalton accepted this stream of meaning when he underlined the distinction between Brahmins, Kshatriyas as well as Sudras and tribals.[67] But Craven tended to be more inclusive when he listed petty traders, blacksmiths, weavers, day-labourers and tenders of village cattle as 'foreigners'.[68]

Empirical understanding that the term *diku* generally meant an exploiting Hindu[69] holds good for Kolhan also. The exploitation was political when it was remarked that crafty local Hindu chieftains conveniently used the Ho for political gains.[70] But later it tended to be cultural in nature when Tickell considered Hindus as a cultural threat to the Ho. He wrote about the simple Hos being 'lured' into adopting their rites, festivals and prejudices. He also held Oriyas responsible for importing cholera, small pox and fevers into Kolhan.[71] Interestingly at the early part of British rule the above criterion did not incorporate the notion of landlord exploitation of Kolhan tribals, which we find in Hoffmann.[72] But later land related exploitation came to be included when Craven noted *diku*s machinating tribal land alienation through the Mankis and Mundas.[73]

Another criterion of meaning was spatial. The governing reason was that the Hodesum or Kolhan being the exclusive Ho country every non-Ho was termed as a foreigner or *diku*. This idea is latent in Roughsedge's ethnic and strangeness notion stated in the earlier section. But perhaps the most affirmative was Ricketts. He wrote in 1854 that Hos would not allow any foreigner to settle in their village except Tantis and Goalas.[74] Here ethnic and space ideas merged as Hindu functional castes were believed to belong to outside. This was why for Dalton 'Diko' meant not only the Hindus but also all those who did not belong to the 'province' of the *Larkas*.[75] This merger was latent in Craven when he considered immigrants from Bihar and Orissa as foreigners.[76] This denotation finds corroboration from Santal Pargana also where a *diku* meant a Bengali of the better class.[77] The above understanding more or less suggested that being situated at the confluence of three provinces of Bengal, Bihar and Orissa Kolhan was subjected to the intrusion of three linguistic and cultural groups. So identification of people of these provinces as *diku*s meant that a *diku* was one who was both demographically and culturally different from the Ho.

Now if we examine whether the difference between Ho and Hindu was essential we come across evidences to the contrary also. First was that the Hos had adopted Hindu rites, festivals and prejudices. Secondly, they had long years of friendly or political relations with local chiefs. Next, we have instances of Brahmins, particularly Oriya, living in Jagannathpur and Jaintgarh, the seats of Porahat raj within Kolhan.[78] Lastly, in the border areas Hos were more prone to Brahmanical influence.[79] These substantiated the reality of on going interaction between Hindu and Ho that disputed not only full segregation of the Hindus, more so upper caste and Hos but also that the Hos invariably put respectable castes to death.

Colonial imperatives as well as increasing knowledge about the demographic relations gradually forced the British to dilute the sharpness of Ho-*diku* hiatus. The dilution started with the Hayes' Settlement (1867) where no prohibitory rule was formulated forbidding the sale of land to a foreigner even when the official knew that no outsider was allowed by Hos to settle in their villages.[80] More significant departure occurred during the Craven Settlement when old *diku*s, i.e. those living in Kolhan before 1867 and their descendants, were bracketed at par with Hos and allowed to own land and pay the same rate of rent as was paid by Hos.[81] While retaining the above criterion of division, during Tuckey Settlement *dikus* were farther classified into desirable and undesirable elements.[82] It meant that the government legalized the immigration of all those who had entered Kolhan after 1867. Not only this, the influx of outsiders, if deemed desirable, was encouraged. Moreover, while owning cultivable land was denied to them, to own uncultivable land was not. In fact, the government was expressly inviting *dikus* as prospectors, miners, forest contractors and traders. So the Chotanagpur Tenancy Act of 1908 provided that the state could take over any land for public purposes i.e. mining operations, construction of official buildings, schools etc.[83]

The flexibility in official policy largely abetted influx of outsiders. Their number steadily grew as these figures show: 1867—24, 313, 1897—69, 399, 1918—97, 978.[84] The trend was that in every Kolhan village a *diku* was found very eager to invite his kin into his village. As a result not only the number of Tantis, Goalas, Kamars and Kumhars rose but also members of the upper caste and Muslims. Some of them were welcome because they served British administration, worked as teachers in local schools and acted as traders, prospectors, miners and forest contractors which helped colonial economy. These outsiders belonged not only to the neighbouring districts and provinces but from other parts of the country also.

The question may yet be raised what the Hos thought of outsiders? Discontent simmered within against *dikus* usurping Ho lands, traders cheating simple Hos at the market places, their marrying or keeping Ho women and also deporting of Ho men or women to Assam by *diku* decoys. Consequently, they had generally an unfavourable image about ethnic outsiders. During *Oteili*, a ceremony connected with land, their *Diuri* or priest uttered 'We will kill the witches, the snakes and the *Dikus*.' This was similar to a Santal comparing a *diku* (Hindu) with a cat and a thorn tree that pricked.[85]

We know of large land transfers and other forms of *diku* exploitation as factors behind *Adivasi* uprisings in Chotanagpur and Santal Parganas.[86] *Sahukar* or liquor-vendor's exploitation caused poverty and indebtedness among tribals of Western India.[87] However, the major irritant was land alienation. We have instances of land transfers through sale and *thika* from a Ho to a non-tribal and some incidence of exploitation by *diku* moneylenders.[88] But the problem could never become as acute in Kohan as in other parts of India mostly because of strict official vigilance. Wilkinson's civil rules and the Chotanagpur Tenancy Act of 1908 played a major role in safeguarding a Ho's land interests.[89] Their grievances being mostly mitigated discontent did not lead to any kind of *diku bhagao* or drive out the *diku*s type of movement. Another factor was that the outsiders were not solely responsible for it as land often passed from a *diku* to a Ho also.[90]

There was yet another dimension to the relation. Over the years increasing *diku* presence in Ho villages, local offices and *hats* developed utilitarian linkages which lessened the hostility of Hos towards outsiders. To substantiate, the Ho imbibed improved agricultural methods from *diku* peasants.[91] *Diku* owned mines gave them employment. *Diku* teachers taught Ho children in schools. At the Kolhan *hats diku* traders supplied them items of daily necessity and purchased their agricultural products. A researcher should take these into account before accepting the British ethnographic portrayal of essential difference between a Ho and *diku*. One should also consider that ethno-spatial cleavage can never be so complete as to compartmentalize two communities living side by side for a long time.

THE MYTH OF MATERIAL PROGRESS

The British in India, more so in Kolhan, considered themselves to be the harbingers of change and development. They created the impression that they were conquering an alien land not for selfish imperialistic gains but for ushering civilization among the Hos. These people were believed to be wild; Kolhan, their land, was an undeveloped jungle tract where state of agriculture was rudimentary and where there was no trade and commerce worth the name.[92] So they thought that it was the bounden duty of the Whiteman to apply the magic touch of British progressivism to set the wild race on a path of moral and material progress. The linearity of progress therefore emerges as the dominant voice from the historical literature.

Since about the 1860s, the material transformation of Kolhan began to characterize British records. The British were confident that three decades of their rule was enough to make a major break. This was variously affirmed. Dalton remarked 'there was every reason to suppose that the people were contented and making fair progress in civilization and prosperity.'[93] In 1883-4, it was reiterated that majority of the people of Singhbhum was well off, food plentiful and cheap, land was abundant and there was no pressure of population on land.[94] Tuckey observed 'since the British occupation, the development of the country has been continuous and rapid.'[95]

What were the markers of progress in the British eyes? First was the visible material change of the Ho who had left nomadism and settled into picturesque villages having a knowledge of alternation of crops.[96] Dalton informed about the extension in area of cultivation and raising of three crops, which enabled the cultivators to pay their revenue with 'utmost punctuality.'[97] Village Papers noted the use of manure and artificial irrigation.[98] The growth of commerce was another sign reflected by the number of weekly *hats* increasing from 24 during 1895-97 to 37 during 1913-18.[99] We learn of an invariable link between a village and near about markets.[100] About the commodities it is related that when outturn of crops was adequate agrarian products were marketed. This resulted in a rise in the price of rice. It sold at 20 seers per rupee in 1878-9, which fell to 7 seers and 9 *chataks* in 1907-8.[101] Moreover, minerals, tassar cocoons, timber and *sabai* grass were major export items from Kolhan.[102] Besides growth in commerce employment opportunities were generated for unskilled labour mostly in the mines. It was claimed that labourers were 'in a position not only to live comfortably for the time being but to put by money which will be available when required for the extension of cultivation and for the many special calls for expenditure.'[103]

The above assertions should however be accepted with a grain of salt. Discordant voices in the midst of continuous trumpeting of all round change and development in official records have to be intercepted in order that more authentic reconstruction of economic history of British-day Kolhan be programmed. Among the early officials, Ricketts seemed perhaps to be the most evaluative. He cryptically commented: 'the Cole of 1854 is a very little improvement on the Cole of 1837'. He then elaborated:

> 'their houses, clothes, food are, with very few exceptions, the same as they were 20 years ago: there is not, so those who knew them say, the remotest token of improvement in their way of living, and the Police reports show that they are as superstitious and savage as ever.'[104]

Both Dalton and the *Note on the History of Singhbhum* observed that Kolhan economy was purely agrarian and materially people were dependent on the out turn of the produce.[105] Now the question is how certain was this out turn? Depending on the vagaries of monsoon agriculture naturally presented a very fluctuating graph. Crop failure led to frequent scarcity causing havoc in life. The failure of winter crop in 1907-8, for example, forced people to live on leaves. Disease sapped the vitality of the people.[106] An escape through trade and commerce was difficult because a Ho produced for his bare needs and he lacked capital and aptitude to become a trader.[107] Moreover, roads were inadequate and poor.[108] Additional development through industrialization was not an official concern. It was officially admitted that till the opening up of the Tata Iron and Steel Company in 1907 Singhbhum was one of the most industrially backward districts of India[109], even when it was perhaps minerally the richest. In the name of factories there were only two shellac factories at Chaibasa.[110] Kolhan had to wait till 1947 for a major industry in the form of the ACC factory at Jhinkpani near Chaibasa.

The colonial policy was mainly to be blamed for this truncated growth. Roads and railways were meant for administration and exports of raw materials from Kolhan. Holding poor condition of roads responsible for commercial backwardness it was observed: 'yet it is well worth opening up the district if only for its forests and wealth of jangal produce'.[111] Besides the government neglect entrepreneurship among the indigenes was missing. They were both allergic and economically backward for any kind of major economic growth or capable of competing with *diku*s. The inevitable result was that while reins of polity were with the British the levers of Kolhan economy gradually passed to outsiders. Not only this, the economic position of common Hos showed a decline. This is evident from two markers. The number of village-wise landless labourers was constantly on the rise.[112] Migration from their hearth and home became a regular feature. People had to move to Mayurbhanj and Keonjhar for agricultural land.[113] The road to Assam tea gardens widened with years as an escape from poverty and starvation.[114] This was perhaps the reality that the myth of material progress hides from an imperceptive observer.

TOWARDS RECONSTRUCTION

This essay has highlighted some of the major generalizations in Ho historiography. We have been deluded to believe that Kolhan was an insulated area; by temperament and habit Ho *Adivasis* were segregationists and invariably a savage and blood-thirsty *Larka*; Kolhan lacked the basic structure and notions of progress and lastly, British rule inaugurated the regime of development in Kolhan. What I seek to argue is that a researcher should identify colonial predilections and prejudices and may attempt reconstruction of an alternate Ho history on a critical study of existing historical literature itself on the following lines.

First, researchers of Ho studies should take their time off from the politico-administrative history, more from the stereotyped study of Ho anti-British uprisings.[115] It is because the extant literature creates the impression that the history of Kolhan began as if with British rule and militancy was the only factor of Ho life. Instead we should underline those areas, which provide more intimate vision of their past. One such area can be the story of their migration and expansion in Singhbhum. Here lies the clue to the gradual emergence of Ho ethnicity from its Munda link. Not only the growth of Ho homogeneity it may provide information about the creation of Ho *killi*s and sub-*killi*s, the fructification of their moral and material culture as well as world view.

The next area may be the history of village making. It will initiate us into the process of their ruralization, when an early settler or *Ham*, chose the village site, demarcated the village area, named it and then invited other members of the lineage or other *killi*s to settle in that village. It is about a Ho developing not only familial but inter-*killi* bonds rather crystallization of the notion of village community. We learn that a village became the centre from which the demographic excess expanded into neighbouring and distant areas to conduct the expansion of *killi* areas, and create a notion of *killi* centres. Perhaps this may also help us to understand whether a *pir* was a political or both political and cultural idea.[116]

The third area is the process of the evolution of Ho socio-economic and religious customs. Such norms of Ho behaviour help appreciate the precise indigenous system, as it evolved over time. While studying the process of formalization of Ho customs into customary law during British rule I encountered paucity of information about their pre-colonial customs. A closer reading of strategic British-day papers may perhaps give us some idea of pre-British Ho culture to enable us to capture the body of customs gradually shaped and moulded during this period.

The concept of *diku* is yet another interesting but unattended area of study[117] requiring independent and detailed researches. It is expected to flesh out the presence of non-Ho elements before the advent of Hos in Singhbhum, influx of outsiders during British rule, the baneful and salutary role of *diku*s in Kolhan, Ho-*diku* interaction and the onset of the process of detribalization and tribalization.

Lastly, a more thorough study of the impact of British rule is necessary. It is because the historical records impress that after initial resistance Hos gradually accepted British paternalism and lived happily under it. But one finds it difficult to explain the abrupt and total conversion of *Larkas* into a docile and loyal community. So the available information should be more critically evaluated to know whether the visible signs of loyalty and Ho supplication was real or it hid the simmering discontent the traces of which are to be found in the records.[118]

Understandably, the literature so far used failed to provide answers to many of our queries on Ho history. But historiographical engagement may be more meaningful if resources are drawn from the Village Papers relating to the Craven and Tuckey Settlements preserved at the District Record Room, Chaibasa. These records of oral evidence and ground experience of villagers and officials lead us into the flow of Ho life around family, *killi* or *hatu*, their sense of homogeneity as well as traces of rupture in them. To reconstruct a more intimate picture of Ho past we shall have however to focus on the story of their mundane life around lineage, family, village community, moral and material culture, concept of power, relations with others etc. We have to draw both on the colonial records as well as oral[119] sources. Perhaps this will lead us nearer that part of their past when Hos were the makers of their own life[120] though the historiographical writings generally tend to dismiss that as uncertain and insignificant.[121] To understand how trivial the indigenes were in colonial perception the study next enters the opening moment of the statist discourse when the imaging of Ho fructified and official policy was formulated.

NOTES

1. British ethnography related the origin of a *pir* to the time when Kolhan was under the control of local chiefs. It was observed that these chiefs had created this unit for the purpose of revenue collection. Tuckey, *Final Report,* p. 13. But this idea should be evaluated in the light of the history of village making. One may possibly argue the existence of trans-village cultural unit on the basis of wider *killi*-centric formations.
2. TSKP of Patajaint, VN 45 Kolhan Thana, pp. 3–7; Ghasiram and Mage Munda's testimony, TSKP of Gamharia, VN 42, p. 2.
3. We have however a collection of songs and legends published during late colonial period. I have no idea whether the temporal origin of the contents and their historical significance has been deciphered. W.G. Archer and B.K. Datta, *Ho Durang: A Ho Song Book*, (Patna, 1942).
4. Lexically generalization is the process of drawing a general conclusion from particular examples or evidences. Since it deals with 'the unique and particular' history is generally criticized as unscientific and incapable of arriving at precise truth. But Carr avers 'It is nonsense to say that generalization is foreign to history; history thrives on generalizations'. Le Goff accords history the status of science when he affirms 'Like any science, therefore, history has to generalize and explain.' Elton characterises generalization as the differentia between the historian and collector of historical facts. To generalize an historian uses the inductive method. This method of logical reason 'obtains or discovers general laws from particular facts or examples.' Correct inference may be drawn only on the basis of law of uniformity of nature and law of causation. An historian's main task is to conceptualize the general from particulars, to find 'general' in the 'unique'. Le Goff calls this 'an internal logic of each element.' But historical method is also that of deduction. We have again Carr in mind: 'The reader, as well as the writer, of history is a chronic generalizer, applying the observation of the historian to other historical contexts with which he is familiar.' Gordon Leff and others are more emphatic when they observe that 'the method of explanation in history is essentially deductive.' In formulating the concept of generalization I have taken help of E.H.Carr, *What is History*, Penguin Books, (1961), pp. 63–4; Jacques Le Goff, *History and Memory*, Columbia University Press, (New York, 1992), p. 121; Oxford Advanced Learner's Dictionary, Fourth Edition, OUP, (Calcutta, 1992), p. 513; John Hospers, *An Introduction to Philosophical Analysis*, Allied Publishers, (New Delhi, 1997), pp. 131–2.
5. Hospers, *An Introduction*, pp. 131–2.
6. The British Ho data bank began with a blank. In 1819, emissaries were sent to collect information about the 'extraordinary race called Larkas' and their country. Dalton, *Tribal History,* pp. 179–80. However, later empirical and interviewed knowledge made significant additions to the corpus. Even

then down to the Tuckey Settlement British understanding of the Hos and their land was not extensive.

7. In 1838-9, out of the rough estimate of Kolhan population of 70,653 about 85 per cent was Ho, the rest were Goalas, Tantis, Lohars and other castes. Tickell, 'Memoir', p. 700.
8. Majumdar, *A Tribe in Transition*, p. 10.
9. Sahu, *The Kolhan,* pp. 1–2.
10. Dalton, *Tribal History,* p. 179.
11. The above territorial ambiguity is largely because of the fact that Tickell, perhaps the only chronicler of this Ho past, collected information from the Oraons and Hos whose memory of the events was very hazy. Tickell, 'Memoir', p. 697.
12. Sahu, *The Kolhan,* p. 266.
13. Craven, *Final Report*, p. 14; Tickell, 'Memoir', p. 700. The fact is that this census conducted on the basis of counting of *hals* could never be scientific.
14. Captain T. Wilkinson to Lt. Tickell, 13 May 1837, para 2. Governor General's Agent, SWFPDR, 13 May to 1 Dececmeber 1840, vol. 231.
15. Tickell, 'Memoir', p. 695.
16. Operations against the Kols in Singboom. Extract Political Letter from Bengal, 9 May 1823, paras 156–7, F/4, 800/21438, Bengal Political Department, OIOC.
17. Samuel Richard Tickell (1811-75) was born in Cuttack. His association with Singhbhum was pretty long. In 1832-33, he was busy quelling the uprising of Ganga Narain. He performed survey work in Kolhan in 1835-36. He then participated in the conquest of Kolhan in 1836-37. Besides first stint as assistant political agent for three years he served in the same capacity from February 1841 to February 1842.
18. Wilkinson to Tickell, 13 May 1837, para 23.
19. Tickell, 'Memoir', p. 803.
20. Dr. W.H. Hayes, Deputy Commissioner of Singhbhum to the Commissioner of Chota Nagpur, No.30, 22 February 1867, p. 128. Revenue Department, June 1867, No. 122.
21. Dalton, *Tribal History,* pp. 177–8.
22. Craven, *Final Report*; Tuckey, *Final Report*.
23. Risley for instance mentioned of the fructification of endogamic distinction among Mundas, Santals and Hos. H.H. Risley, *The Tribes and Castes of Bengal*, vol. I, (Calcutta, 1981), pp. 319–20. Second was the identification of Kolhan Kols as Ho *jat* (caste) during Tuckey Settlement. Tuckey Settlement, U/S 85 Village Papers give details of familial/individual land holdings. Ho tenants had been noted as belonging to Ho *jat* (caste).
24. E. Roughsedge, Agent to the Governor General, to Lt. Col. James Nicol, Adjutant General, 31 March 1820, paras 1-2, No. 109, Extract Bengal Political Consultations, 15 April 1820; Roughsedge to Mr. Secretary Metcalfe, 9 May 1820, para 7, No. 38, Extract Bengal Political Consultations, 3 June 1820.

25. Tickell, 'Memoir', p. 694.
26. Hayes to the Commissioner of Chotanagpur, p. 128; Dalton, *Tribal History*, p. 163; Craven, *Final Report*, p. 19.
27. Craven, *Final Report*, pp. 20–3, 29, 32; Tuckey, *Final Report*, pp. 5-6, 8, 17.
28. Roughsedge to Metcalfe, 9 May 1820, para 7.
29. Tickell, 'Memoir', p. 697.
30. Roughsedge to Nicol, 31 March 1820, para 2; Roughsedge to Metcalfe, 9 May 1820, para 12.
31. Roughsedge to Metcalfe, 9 May 1820, paras 16–8.
32. Roughsedge to Nicol 31 March 1820, para 10; Roughsedge to Metcalfe, 9 May 1820, paras 20–7.
33. Sahu, *The Kolhan*, pp. 70–81.
34. Dalton, *Tribal History*, p. 194.
35. Such a shift is visible in a recent essay where the conspiracy theory and role of the loyalist Hos have virtually diluted the other side of the picture. Sanjukta Das Gupta, 'Rebellion in a "Little-Known" District', pp. 99, 111–2.
36. Tickell, 'Memoir', p. 807.
37. Bradley-Birt, *Chotanagpur*, pp. 85–6.
38. Tickell, 'Memoir', pp. 696–7.
39. Dalton, *Tribal History*, pp. 177, 185.
40. Roughsedge to Metcalfe, 9 May 1820, para 13.
41. Tickell, 'Memoir', p. 803.
42. Dalton, *Tribal History*, pp. 177, 184–5.
43. Tuckey, *Final Report*, pp. 8, 22–3.
44. S.C. Roy, *The Mundas and their Country*, Asia Publishing House, (Calcutta, 1970), Chapter II.
45. This they could do through an understanding with Bhuiyans and the Singh *rajas* of Porahat as well as after a fight with Saraks. Tickell, 'Memoir', pp. 696–7.
46. S. Guha, 'Lower Strata, Older Races, and Aboriginal Peoples: Racial Anthropology and Mythical History Past and Present', *The Journal of Asian Studies*, 57, no.2, (May 1998), pp. 424–8, 436.
47. N.K. Bose, *Tribal Life in India*, National Book Trust, India, (New Delhi, 1990), pp. 1–4.
48. Roughsedge to Metcalfe, 9 May 1820, para 7.
49. Tickell, 'Memoir', p. 698. It has been impressed that simple and juvenile Hos had been duped by local chiefs to join them. This notion denies Hos of the rationality to take independent decisions.
50. Roughsedge to Metcalfe, 9 May 1820, para 16.
51. Tickell, 'Memoir', p. 805.
52. Ibid., p. 803.
53. Ibid., pp. 797–8.
54. Dalton, *Tribal History*, p. 185.

55. TSVN, for report about village-wise break up of Ho and non-Ho population.
56. See Tuckey Settlement Village Papers.
57. Craven Settlement papers of Tangar Pokharia and Parampancha villages.
58. TSVN, for village-wise data.
59. TSKP of Khairpal, pp. 3–10, VN 44; Tanaza papers of Gangda, pp. 4–6, VN 1 of Manoharpur Thana.
60. TSKP of Danguaposhi and Baihatu and Dikuponga village under Manoharpur thana.
61. Tuckey, *Final Report,* p. 128.
62. M. Areeparampil, 'Socio-Cultural and Religious movements', pp. 396–436.
63. Chaudhuri, 'Auponiveshik Purba Bharate Hindu-Adivasi Sanskritik Samparka', pp. 150–1.
64. Sinha, Sen and Panchabhai, 'The Concept of Diku', pp. 121–4.
65. Dalton called Kolhan an exclusive Ho territory. He knew about non-Ho settlements but his knowledge was very cursory. Dalton, *Tribal History,* p. 185. Tickell similarly related about Goalas, Tantis, Lohars and other castes residing in Kolhan without any further information about them. Tickell, 'Memoir', p. 700.
66. In this connection I would like to draw readers' attention to two evocative observations: "Colonizer's knowledge of the colonized was not and could never be neutral to the relation of dominance and subordination." R. Guha's Introduction in B.S. Cohn, *An Anthropologist among Historians and other Essays*, OUP, (Delhi, 1990), p. ix and "knowledge was what colonialism was all about." Foreword by N.B. Dirks in B.S. Cohn, *Colonialism and its forms of Knowledge*, p. 3.
67. Dalton, *Tribal History,* pp. 164–7, 185. This distinction generally prevailed in other parts of Chotanagpur also. Sinha, Sen and Panchabhai, pp. 124–5.
68. Craven, *Final Report,* pp. 20–3.
69. Sinha, Sen & Panchabhai, 'The Concept', pp. 121–3.
70. Wilkinson to Tickell, 13 May 1837, paras 7, 16, 24.
71. Tickell, 'Memoir', pp. 706, 803–7.
72. By *diku* he meant a Hindu, Hindu landlord and then the linguistic group speaking Hindi or Sadani. Sinha, Sen & Panchabhai, p. 122.
73. Craven, *Final Report,* p. 21.
74. H. Ricketts, *Report on the district of Singhbhum, vide Selections from the Records of the Bengal Government*, No. XVI, (Calcutta, 1854), para 109.
75. Dalton, *Tribal History*, pp. 167, 169.
76. Craven, *Final Report,* pp. 20–3.
77. Sinha, Sen & Panchabhai, 'The Concept', p. 122.
78. For Brahmin presence see TSKP of Tangar Pokharia, Jugi Nanda, *Diku* Balkand, Jaintgarh and Jagannathpur.
79. Tickell, 'Memoir', p. 803.
80. Craven, *Final Report,* pp. 30–1.

81. As against them those immigrating into Kolhan after 1867 were called new *dikus*. Their rate of rent was double the normal. Ibid., pp. 8–22, 29–31.
82. Tuckey, *Final Report,* pp. 22–6.
83. S.N. Datta, *The Chotanagpur Tenancy Act*, (Patna, 1928), section 50 (1), p. 114.
84. Sahu, *The Kolhan,* p. 266.
85. Sinha, Sen & Panchabhai, 'The Concept', p. 127.
86. Besides J.C. Jha, *The Tribal Revolt of Chotanagpur* (*1831-32*), K.P. Jayaswal Research Institute, (Patna, 1987) and R.Guha, *Elementary Aspects*, the problem can be studied from M.C. McAlpin, *Report on the condition of the Sonthals in the Districts of Birbhum, Bankura, Midnapore and North Balasore*, (Calcutta, 1981), pp. 24–41.
87. Hardiman, *The Coming of the Devi*, Chapters 6 and 7.
88. Craven and Tuckey Settlement village-wise papers for *thika* recordings and also *Diku* Reports.
89. It should however be pointed out that in the name of supposed development land in Kolhan was transferred to individuals and Companies for which clauses 49 and 50 of the CNT Act could be invoked. Such instances are available in Craven and Tuckey Settlement village related papers.
90. Craven and Tuckey Settlement village-wise papers for *thika* recordings and also *Diku* Reports.
91. Sahu, *The Kolhan,* p. 207.
92. Tickell, 'Memoir', p. 804.
93. Dalton, *Tribal History*, p. 183.
94. GAR for 1883-4, Singhbhum district (top cover missing, no further details), para 17.
95. Tuckey, *Final Report,* p. 10.
96. Hayes to the Commissioner of Chotanagpur, p. 130.
97. Dalton, *Tribal History,* pp. 183, 195.
98. See Tuckey Settlement Village Notes.
99. Tuckey, *Final Report,* p. 3.
100. Tuckey Settlement Village Notes.
101. GAR for 1878-9, No. 678, Chaibasa, May 1879, p. 8; LRAR for 1908-9, DC's office, RD, CN XI Returns, FN 10 of 1908-9, Appendix XXIX.
102. Craven, *Final Report,* p. 15.
103. Note on the history of Singhbhum district during the decade 1901-11, pp. 17–8 (page numbering by the author), FL, CN VII, FN 25 of 1911-12.
104. Ricketts, *Report,* pp. 74, 92.
105. Dalton, *Tribal History*, p. 196; Note on the history, p. 14.
106. Note on the history, p. 6.
107. Tickell, 'Memoir', p. 804; LRAR for 1910-11, DC's office, RD, CN XI, FN 3 of 1910-11, para XLIX.
108. GAR, 1883-4, p. 30. Up to 1883-4 there were only 533 miles of road in Singhbum district, Ibid., p. 126.

109. Note on the history, p. 29.
110. Ibid., p. 30.
111. GAR, 1878-9, p. 31.
112. Craven and Tuckey Settlement papers may be perused.
113. LRAR for 1907-8, DC's office, RD, CN XI Returns, FN 16, para 21. See also LRAR for 1910-11.
114. *See* the last chapter.
115. I have in mind C.P. Singh and Sahu's books which make a stereotyped narration of events, which fail to focus on the nature of uprisings, modes of mobilization or shades of militancy as against the insightful studies of peasant insurgency in Guha's *Elementary Aspects* or R. Samaddar's evocative suggestions in *Memory, Identity, Power: Politics in the Jungle Mahals (West Bengal), 1890-1950*, Sangam Books, (London, 1998), particularly pp. 72–3. S. Dasgupta's essay on 'Adivasi Politics in Midnapore, c 1760-1924', *Subaltern Studies* IV, OUP, Delhi 1990, pp. 101–35 is another useful study
116. We learn of *pir* being a legacy of royal rule. Its birth has been assigned to local chiefs' policy of appropriating revenue through Mankis or heads of *pirs*. Tuckey, *Final Report*, p. 13.
117. Sinha, Sen & Panchbhai's study is a useful field-study. But it is not historically informed. Moreover, it lacks the focus on Ho. Sahu broaches only one aspect of the problem of *diku* i.e. land alienation. *The Kolhan*, pp. 138–48.
118. See 'Singhbhum 1927-30' and for more information Papers on forest preserved at DRCC.
119. Recent writings while underlining the centrality of oral narrative in appropriating tribal past also emphasize on interaction between oral and literate sources. Sivaramakrishnan, *Modern Forests,* pp. 18-19; Skaria, *Hybrid Histories*, pp. 7, 19; R.C. Heredia, 'Tribal History: Living Word or Dead Letter', *Economic and Political Weekly*, Vol. XXXV, No. 18, April 29, 2000, p. 1522.
120. This autonomy of subaltern consciousness has been forcefully argued by R. Guha, 'The Prose of Counter-Insurgency', *Subaltern Studies* II, OUP, (Delhi, 1983), p. 33.
121. That an *Adivasi* past was uncertain is suggested by H.H. Risley in their inadequacy to retain it properly, *The Tribes and Castes of Bengal*, p. 225 and the critique of the lack of past itself by S. Guha, 'Lower Strata', p. 431 and Hardiman, *The Coming of the Devi*, p. 13.

4

Roughsedge's Equation and the Notion of Savage: Towards the Threshold of British Tribal Policy in Singhbhum

'In fact the terms the settler uses when he mentions the native are zoological terms...When the settler seeks to describe the native fully in exact terms he constantly refers to the bestiary'
—Frantz Fenon, *The Wretched of the Earth*

Major E. Roughsedge[1] was the leader of the British army engaged in subduing the Ho during 1819-20. His experiences, as reported in his letter of 9 May 1820 to C.T. Metcalfe, the Secretary to the Government, contained his historic observation about the *Larka* Kols. To quote 'A traveller would as soon think of venturing into a tiger's den as of traversing any point of Larka Cole.'[2]

This chapter seeks to examine the above statement by applying historico-analytical[3] methodology to instance how British ethnographer-administrators formed judgments that determined the content of colonial ethnography. The broad argument is that the generalized statement like the one under review was neither a harmless rhetoric nor a semantic slip by a British general but it offers an insight into colonial representation of the Ho, rather the indigenes in general. Divided into two major sections the essay first explores how the given equation originated and how this analytical technique may help us critically examining the very process of judgment making, some of which have been questioned in earlier chapter. The second briefly outlines how on the mythic characterization of the society under review the British tribal policy was subsequently formulated and an inadequate ethnography constructed. By challenging many of the accepted notions about the indigenes in British-day ethnography the methodology may in the end prove historiographically inversive. But the authors argue that even then it should be deployed for evaluating archival evidences and revising our understanding of the historical situation.[4]

GENESIS OF THE EQUATION: ROUGHSEDGE'S HERITAGE

The British contact with Singhbhum and the people known as the *Larka* Kols began in 1767. In a petition to George Vansittart, the resident of Midnapur, *raja* Jagannath Singh of Porahat sought British help against his cousin Sheonath Singh and the *Larkas*. The resident could learn that the Kols termed as 'a tribe of plundering banditti' had allegedly gained control over a sizeable number of villages belonging to the *raja*. In fact, out of a total of 14,000 villages in Singhbhum, only 500 were then under *raja*'s possession while most of the remaining were with the *Larkas*.[5] In 1768, Vansittart deputed two sepoys to collect information about the *Larkas* and their area as well as the extent of the Maratha's control over this region. But the mission failed, as the emissaries could not penetrate more than a *kos*[6] beyond the frontier. Failing in this effort the British targeted the chiefs of Singhbhum. They first launched an attack on Dhalbhum in 1773 and forced the *raja* of Dhalbhum to execute an obligation not to harbour merchants for transporting salt through his territory in future. Twenty years later the East India Company government compelled the chiefs of Seraikela and Kharsawan to sign an agreement promising not to provide shelter to any fugitive rebels from the British territories.[7] During the second Anglo-Maratha war (1803-6), Lord Wellesley, the Governor General, invited the chief of Seraikela to render help to the British. In return the government promised to honour his right to hold his territory free of revenue. The English however made no further attempt to enter into relations with the chiefs of Singhbhum. So the territories dominated by the *Larkas* continued to remain a closed land for them.[8]

ROUGHSEDGE'S INTERCOURSE

The remoteness decreased in subsequent years as the British gradually gained further knowledge about the land and its people. At this stage Roughsedge's intercourse, first indirect and then direct, with the

Larkas began. On 30 May 1809, he reported to Edmonstone, the Secretary to the Company government, about the rapidly dwindling power and territory of the *raja* of Porahat due to the growing power of the *Larkas* as well as the chiefs of Seraikela and Kharsawan.[9] Obviously, it was the *raja* of Porahat who passed this information to the British. This he did to procure British military help to subjugate his adversaries. The Company government, which had spurned similar overtures of the Porahat raj in 1767 and 1809, could no longer remain indifferent. After their victory in the third Anglo-Maratha war in 1818 imperialist motives prompted the British to intervene. This brought Roughsedge in the scene occasioning his direct contact and setting the situation for the formation of his equation.

Roughsedge directed his assistant Lt. Ruddel in 1819 to proceed to Porahat to negotiate a settlement with the chief and collect all possible information regarding the country and particularly the 'extraordinary race called Larka'. The assistant, however, failed to forge any contact with these people.[10] But in January-February 1820, *kunwar* Bikram Singh of Seraikela, *thakur* Chaitan Singh of Kharsawan and *raja* Ghanashyam Singh of Porahat entered into agreements with the British and subjected themselves under the protection of the Company government.[11] Ghanashyam forged this alliance to bring the *Larkas* under his control with the English help. Roughsedge was initially unwilling to render any assistance. But soon he felt compelled to protect people of the *parganas* of Sonepur, Bilreagarh and Bussea in Chotanagpur from the inroads of these 'savages'.[12]

The restoration of peace and order however was not the only motive. Another compulsion was to keep the road safe and free in the *Larka pirs* and to provide free passage to travellers.[13] Before his military operations began, Roughsedge had access to further information about the *Larkas*. He learnt from the chiefs of Singhbhum that for the last fifty years they 'had thrown off all appearance of subordination to the *Rajah* (Ghanashyam Singh) and other chieftains of Singhbhoom.'[14] Probably at this time the English general could learn that the strength and power of the *Larkas* drew on their earlier military achievements. Between 1770 and 1800 AD, they successfully thwarted the attempts made, first by Drupnath Sahi, the grandfather of the then zamindar of Chotanagpur at the head of 20,000 men, assisted by the troops of *raja* of Singhbhum, secondly, by *raja*

Jagannath Singh with almost an equal number of force and lastly by the zamindar of Bamanghatty, to subjugate them. The enemies were repulsed with heavy losses of men and material. The second battle, details of which were related by an eyewitness, Roughsedge learnt that hundreds of *raja*'s troops were killed and several died during the enemies' 'long chase for ten miles'.[15] So the British general was fully acquainted with the enormity and seriousness of the task he had undertaken.

At the head of a battalion of artillery, cavalry and infantry, Roughsedge reached Seraikela on 20 February 1820. Initially, he adopted conciliatory and peaceful means to bring the *Larkas* into submission. Though the Mundas of Ajudhia and Rajabassa *pirs* could be conciliated, the others tactically allowed the British troops to advance unmolested into the heart of their country. After they encamped at Chaibasa, the tribesmen began their counter-attack. Sometimes open and at times guerilla warfare with bows, arrows and battle-axes, with dare devilry the British had seldom experienced in India before, the *Larkas* forced the enemy to fight for every inch's advance. When left no room for fight they escaped into the fastness of the hills and jungles. The British retaliated with indiscriminate arson, loot and murder. This brought in its trail gradual surrender of villages before the remorseless march of the mightier British military machine.[16] At last the entire *Larka* land capitulated and accepted the overlordship of the *raja* of Singhbhum which it was Roughsedge's mission to achieve. But the entire process took almost two months. The gruesome experience convinced the English that they had met their match in the open fields, hills and jungles of Singhbhum. This experience prompted the General to report to his superior 'A traveller would as soon think of venturing into a tiger's den as of traversing any point of Larka Cole.'

Before analyzing the above equation it is perhaps pertinent to broach the broad content of the above letter. Understandably this correspondence from the battlefield concentrated on the military operations. But the reason why this letter may claim a high place in early British Ho ethnography is the quantum of information about the land and people, particularly about Ho life and their attitude towards the *diku*, that it contains. To quote.

> 'Not having any of the feelings of veneration for Bramins, cows which pervade Hindoos of every description they make

> no scruple of putting to death any man of respectable caste who presumes to enter their territory, nor is there I can venture to affirm a single Bramin, Rajpoot or Mussulman in any one of the numerous and well inhabited villages they possess. A traveller would as soon think of venturing into tiger's den as of traversing any point of Lurka Cole'.

The above statement first relates that the Ho considered themselves different from the Hindus in their disregard both for the Brahmin and cow who were generally venerated by the former. This information may be taken as a proof of their distinct cultural identity. But this aspect of Ho self-imaging has not been taken up here for lack of space. What this chapter seeks to emphasize is the territorial sensibility of the Ho which inspired their hostility towards outsiders epitomized in the above equation. But the question that may naturally arise in our mind is to what extent the above statement is factually corroborated in the above letter. More so it is necessary to assess how far the correspondence between a tiger and *Larka*, which has been developed below, has been logically drawn. This has necessitated the following historico-analytical test.

ANALYSIS OF THE EQUATION

Identity of the Traveller

Roughsedge's equation contains three key terms (1) traveller (2) tiger's-den (3) point-of-*Larka* Kol. A semantic clarification of these three terms is necessary for providing a precise understanding of the identity. Of these three, (2) and (3) indicate the geographical spaces that a tiger and *Larka* Kol occupied, while (1) is primarily a demographic category. Lexically, the word traveller means 'one who travels or has travelled', 'a wayfarer'. As such the act of travelling is the defining characteristic of the word traveller. It has also an accompanying characteristic, namely strangeness. The space a traveller first moves into is strange, so is he/she to the place/people travelled to. So travelling implies in a sense strangeness also.[17]

The spatio-demographic identity of the traveller helps to indicate the relationship of difference between the traveller-category and *Larka* Kol-category as well as traveller-space and *Larka* Kol-space. However, vagueness of the term can be removed by providing the clearer understanding of the term traveller. In this exercise the accompanying characteristic i.e. strangeness tends to become defining. So traveller is more or less substituted by stranger as we seek a more precise meaning. This will also help to correct Roughsedge's error in the use of the term.

When the traveller accosted the *Larka* land his strangeness might be one of physical look, skin colour, speech and dress. These parameters of strangeness did not obviously relate a tribal traveller because of the similarity of physical look, skin colour, speech and dress. Immediacy of strangeness due to the ethnic traveller not belonging to the neighbourhood would be mellowed further by the observance of the same customs and rituals. This feeling of homogeneity either at inter-village or inter-*pir* level meant that a tribal traveller with immediacy of strangeness could ultimately be identified to belong to the same ethnic group obviating thereby any fear of physical harm. So the demographic and spatial identity of the traveller could be that the person was ethnically different and did not belong to the tribal area. From the letter it becomes clear that Roughsedge meant that he was none other than the Brahmin, Rajput and Mussalman, rather any person of reputable caste irrespective of his geographical locus.

Larka-tiger Equivalence

The proposition 'A traveller would as soon think of venturing into a tiger's den as of traversing any point of Larka Cole' suggested that like tiger's den *Larka* Kol point also portended physical harm and death to a traveller. Paraphrased the sentence may stand as: if a traveller traversed any point of *Larka* Kol, he would immediately think of venturing into a tiger's den. This is the formulation of a relation of equivalence. First it means the equivalence between two spaces i.e. tiger's den and *Larka* Kol point. It implies man-animal equivalence or equivalence between a tiger and *Larka* Kol. Next, the equation also formulates the notion of distance or hostility between a traveller's space and *Larka* Kol's space and between a traveller i.e. stranger and a *Larka* Kol. A stranger would prefer to avoid the point of *Larka* Kol because of tiger-*Larka* Kol identity or tigerliness of a *Larka* Kol.

The Equation and Positive Instances

In Roughsedge's perception a *Larka* Kol thus corresponded a tiger and as such he was ferocious to any stranger. This section next investigates the supportive instances on which the equation was inferred. We will first examine how in his perception a Ho corresponded a tiger. A tiger is a wild animal. Lexically the term wild means one in a state of nature, undomesticated, uncivilized and fierce. For the *Larkas* of Ajudhia *pir*, which formed the northern most *taluk* of the *Larka* territory, Roughsedge used the epithet 'wild inhabitants.'[18] Savage, which also verbally means one in a state of nature, wild, uncivilized, a human being in a wild or primitive state, is the other word more frequently used. It is observed 'the savages with a degree of rashness and foolhardiness.'[19] Wild-savage concept being defined by fierceness and ferociousness, this particular parameter seems to have next been applied to bracket tiger and *Larka* categories together. Ferocity is suggested through the narration of incidence of attack, destruction and slaughter by the *Larkas*.[20] What is amusing is that even the exemplary courage vindicated by the tribesmen defying the fear of physical harm and death came to reinforce the colonial representation further. Roughsedge wrote 'these savages with a degree of rashness and foolhardiness which scarcely credible met the charge of the troop, half way in open plain battle axe in hand.'[21] In this quotation the crucial words are 'savage', 'rashness' and 'foolhardiness.' In their exact sequence these words create the notion of causation. A *Larka* was savage, so he was rash and foolhardy. This incredible rashness and foolhardiness meant that a *Larka* was irrational, implying him thereby to be a non-human. Tiger correspondence had other visible symbols also. After attack they escaped into the fastness of hills and jungles.[22] The next is deportation or carrying off of cattle, particularly buffaloes by them[23], likeable to a tiger's escape with the spoil.

Now let us look for the evidences on the basis of which Roughsedge might have inferred tigerliness of a *Larka* vis-à-vis the traveller i.e. stranger i.e. non-tribe i.e. respectable caste. The *Larka*-non-tribe implied a dichotomous relation which had a spatio-demographic implication. Taking up space aspect first, we notice that the polarity was very sharp and total as made out by Roughsedge. He informed 'all travellers make a circuit of twenty miles to the east to avoid these dreaded savages.'[24] Obviously, borrowing the information from Roughsedge, Dalton later revealed who this traveller could be. He wrote 'The Hos would allow no stranger to settle in or even to pass through the Kolhan, and pilgrims to Jagannath (Puri) had to make a circuit of several days journey to avoid it.'[25] So here traveller-stranger meant people (Hindus) belonging to distant space who even avoided an entry into tribal land, what to think of settling, for fear of physical harm in Kolhan. This indicates total ethnic polarity between *Larka* Kol and non-tribal from distant space.

What about non-tribal of the neighbourhood? The Porahat raj, who claimed themselves to be of Mewar Rajput descent, had been ruling since the 13th century AD.[26] But the *Larkas* 'had thrown off all appearance of subordination to the *Rajah* and other chieftains of Singhbhoom.'[27] They carried raids with impunity into the territories of Singhbhum (Porahat, Seraikela and Kharsawan) and Orissa chieftains indulging in excesses.[28] As a result they were so afraid of the power and ferocity of these people that they 'trembled at the thought of penetrating into the county of the Larkas.'[29] Since the battle between Jagannath Singh and the *Larkas* about fifty years ago, the chief of Seraikela was forced to abandon the populous and well-maintained *pir* of Rajabassa.[30] Jaintgarh Brahmins, the hereditary descendants of the ancient *killedar* of Jaintgarh, had earned persona-non-grata status vis-à-vis the tribesmen and lived a life of constant hazard and trepidation.[31] These summed up the positive instances which seemed to have reasoned Roughsedge's judgment.

The Equation and Negative Instances

Now the question is whether the judgment inductively drawn on the basis of above supportive evidences in the letter may be internally and externally critiqued. Interestingly, a close perusal informs of contrary data that renders its position contingent rather than necessary. The idea of wild and savage is challenged by many such marks of civilized life as 'numerous and well inhabited villages'[32]; 'the singular spectacle of well-cultivated...country studded with large villages'[33]; 'their well-cultivated fields and villages abounding in sheep, goats, fowls and pigs'[34]; 'village administration through the Mundas and Mankis'[35]; and prevalence of monogamy and marriage when both sexes attained puberty.[36] The above marks of civilization strangely did not qualify the *Larkas* to be classed as the civilized i.e. non-savage. What seems probable is that Roughsedge chose to deviate from the lexical meaning of the term civilized. So in spite of the attainment of an organized communal life depicting advance in material culture they were termed as 'ferocious and sanguinary'[37] people i.e. uncultivated or savage. To be precise Roughsedge's civilization-criterion was not advance in material culture but avoidance of aggression and hostility, to further explicate 'predatory and lawless' behaviour.[38] It means that avoidance of predatoriness-lawlessness has been used here as the defining characteristic of civilization. It may not be out of place to point out that ferocity was not exclusively a tribal preserve because even the civilized British also indulged in terrible acts of barbarity to subjugate the *Larkas*.[39]

The necessariness of tribe-non-tribe (both respectable and others) dichotomy can similarly be contended by supplying dissenting evidences of continued existentialist link between the *Larka* and non-tribals belonging both to contiguous and distant places. First the link was political. Instances in support were that populous and well-maintained Rajabassa *pir* was under the possession of the ancestors of Bikram Singh about half a century ago[40] and next the *taluk* of sixty villages named Bantera was formerly a *khash* possession of the *raja*.[41] We learn that in spite of the supportive instance rupture of relations was not permanent, the tribesmen continued to honour and respect the Singh chiefs as allies though not as rulers.[42] Next was cultural as shown by the habitations of Brahmins in Jaintgarh, the principal seat of the *raja* of Porahat's power on the southern side of Singhbhum[43] and the presence of *Pahuns* (weavers), *Goalas* (herdsmen) and *Kamhars* (blacksmiths) in tribal villages.[44] The relations seemed to be much extensive if we take into account commercial link between Kolhan and Puri for salt and visit of merchants from outside to purchase tassar cocoons. But the cultural contact was perhaps more deep-rooted as the Hos were found acculturating themselves to Hindu 'ceremonies, rites, festivals and prejudices' and tribals of the border areas were under the influence of Brahmins.[45]

FORMULATION OF THE TRIBAL POLICY

The above historico-logical analysis of the equation shows that Roughsedge inferred inductively on the basis of part of reality by taking into consideration only the favourable instances, while conveniently avoiding negative ones and elevating his conclusion to the status of general truth. This bias seems to have been inspired by the colonialist British assumption of its essential link with civilization and the antonymic image of the colonized in his mind. On this basis Roughsedge castigated the *Larka* as uncivilized because they had opposed the British i.e. civilization itself. This inspired him to ignore the apparent marks of advance in material culture made by them. One may like to debate that his formulation was more an exercise at figurative use of language than the enumeration of reality. But what we notice is that Roughsedge's polemic on the tribe and the subsequent fructification of the savage-tiger image by him impacted colonial policy of demographic polarity. No less significant it also considerably influenced the process of colonial knowledge-making.

The British followed the policy of demographic polarization. Accordingly, the Ho were divided as friendly and refractory, the people of Singhbhum both as the non-tribe and tribe as well as civilized and non-civilized.[46] This policy was also selectively used to suit the imperatives of British administration. The intra-*Larka* distinction into friendly and refractory, depending on which side a *Larka* belonged, was practised only to strengthen their position during tribal movements of 1819-21, 1836-7 and 1857-8. After 1858 as the *Larka* Kols finally surrendered to British rule this dichotomy was deleted from the British diplomatic programme. On the other hand, though the ethnic distinction between tribe and non-tribe, rather Ho and non-tribe, continued to be a permanent British policy, it was mellowed down by the imperatives of British colonialism. We do not however continue the discussions further as this has been more or less elaborated in an earlier essay.[47]

The third policy of forging the distinction of civilized and non-civilized was however the main part of Roughsedge's equation. While the two above were guided by the logic of divide and rule this more or less served the British agenda of civilizing the Ho. One should however remember that by formulating cultural distinction between the civilized others and animalish Ho Roughsedge anticipated the 'Social Darwinists' who believed that primitiveness of tribals must be replaced by so-called modern civilization.[48] The basic premise was that the British were the torchbearers of civilization into a supposed dark and wild country. The Ho *Adivasis* rightly deserved British attention, as they were wild, wildness being reflected by their savagery, raids, shifting cultivation and absence of centralized polity. So to civilize them it was necessary to gradually bring them under a centralized and well-regulated British polity[49], and then their mind and body had to be cured through western education and medicine.

With this aim in mind the East India Company introduced western rules and regulations and founded an administrative system which incorporated the indigenous Manki-Munda and *panchayat* systems into the *Raj* framework.[50] Secondly, policy of introducing the market economy was formulated by opening weekly market at Chaibasa and encouraging traders from outside to settle in Kolhan. Besides the material gain, it was believed that by inducting 'the Kols' to attend a weekly market they would become more civilized through contact with the 'sepahis and other Hindus'.[51] Since then the bedrock of British tribal policy was the continuous and widening exposure of Singhbhum tribals to the market economy. The growing number of *hats* and villagers carting miles to the weekly market places were considered the sure signs of Kolhan tribals being incorporated in exotic economy.[52]

Civilizing the wild required induction of other idioms of culture. The British found that wildness of the *Larkas* did not end simply with their hostility to outsiders but it was equally driven towards the self when they indulged in indiscriminate killing of their own people on the charge of witchcraft. Perhaps Roughsedge did not have the sufficient empirical knowledge about witch murder as inflating the inventory of *Larka* savagery. But we notice that about two decades later learning that witch killing was a pervasive anomaly in Ho society Wilkinson instructed his assistant Tickell to take appropriate measures for its eradication. What seems interesting however is that he instructed his subordinate to treat the problem as a deep-seated mental prejudice, rather than as a mere law and order aberration, cure of which lay in the change of mind rather than through apprehension and punishment.[53]

Wilkinson learnt that the 'Kols' attributed their sickness to witchcraft and displeasure of their *bongas* and spirits. They believed that they could cure witchcraft only by eliminating the suspected with all the members of his/her family. Obviously British officials rejected what the Ho community considered to be the cure of illness. Instead they prescribed first that members of the suspected or socially supposed witches be removed to a village where such a prejudice did not exist against them. And next that physical ailment should be subjected to treatment by 'our medicine' (Western/ British) by sending the sick to a hospital proposed to be opened at Chaibasa.[54] At the same time they also rightly believed that panacea of the evil was western education, which Wilkinson averred would remove 'the dreadful prejudice' of witchcraft completely. We should understand that the Bentinck-day administrator was prescribing the same medicine, which his peer did by emphasizing western education as the panacea for Indian social evils. So physical and mental treatment i.e. policies regarding health and education charted their course in Singhbhum as ancillary, a concomitant to the greater strategy of the reform of witchcraft. This marginality was eloquent in the palpably inadequate health and education facilities provided for Singhbhum during the entire length of British rule.[55] This also impacted the process of knowledge-making.

Representation of the indigenes in mainstream episteme[56] was governed basically by the ethno-centrism of western knowledge-makers who conceived and practised binaries of western and non-western societies.[57] The people classified as state/pre-state, literate/ oral and historied/historiless societies[58] structured the distinction between the civilized and the uncivilized. In this scale pre-state 'constitution of confederate village communities' or republics, of the *Larkas* without having the notion of a centralized government[59] or their Ho dialect reinforced the colonial argument that being essentially uncivilized they were historiless, rather people not worthy to be historicized. The sum total of this attitude was that 'uncivilized' and 'savage' people were considered epistemically dispensable. The net result was that the British ethnographers did not appear to be serious enough to appropriate knowledge beyond the needs of the governance. Next this quest was conditioned also by the mindset that as the Ho rather the indigenes had stepped into history after the onset of British rule the traces of pre-colonial past[60], which they had an access to during empirical investigation, were generally left unexplored. This finally caused epistemic denial of the Ho in mainstream historiography to remove which the quest of newer source materials like the one invoked in the next chapter is deemed very necessary. With this I now move from the perusal of the statist source relating largely to the early phase of British rule to almost its last phase when the colonial policy had fructified to its logical end and had remade the ruled space and people under review.

NOTES

1. Fighting Kols, more preferably Hos, which the tribe of this name prefer themselves to be called.
2. Roughsedge to Metcalfe, 9 May 1820, para 15.
3. This methodology has drawn on the philosophical analytical technique developed in Hospers, *An Introduction to Philosophical Analysis*.
4. I cull Hayden White in support who considers an understanding of 'the essentially provisional and contingent nature of historical representations and of their susceptibility to infinite revision in the light of new evidence or more sophisticated conceptualization of problems' as one of the marks of a good professional historian. Hayden White, *Tropics of Discourse*, p. 82.
5. McPherson, *Final Report*, p. 18.
6. A *kos* means two miles.
7. O'Malley, *Bengal District Gazetteer*, pp. 31–2.
8. Ibid., p. 32.
9. Major Roughsedge to J. Adam, Chief Secretary, 12 May 1818, vide Singh, *Ho Tribe of Singhbhum*, p. 62.
10. Dalton, *Tribal History*, p. 180.
11. Sahu, *The Kolhan*, p. 20.
12. Roughsedge to Metcalfe, 9 May 1820, paras 10–1.
13. Ibid., paras 22, 33.
14. Ibid., para 9.
15. Ibid., para 17.
16. Ibid., paras 25–31; E. Roughsedge to Lt. Nicol, Adjutant General, 31 March 1820, paras 2–11, 9 April 1820, paras 1-2, SWFPDR, 6 October 1819–10 November 1820, Vol. XXVI; Dalton, *Tribal History*, pp. 181–2.
17. Probably on the basis of Roughsedge's information Dalton repeated the same idea but substituted traveller with stranger i.e. stranger being accepted as a synonym for traveller. Dalton, *Tribal History*, p. 179.
18. Roughsedge to Nicol, 31 March 1820, para 2.
19. Ibid., paras 4, 30 and also Roughsedge to Metcalfe, 9 May 1820, para 11.
20. Roughsedge to Nicol, paras 2, 6, 16 and Roughsedge to Metcalfe, para 12.
21. Roughsedge to Nicol, para 4.
22. Ibid., paras 3–4.
23. Roughsedge to Metcalfe, paras 12, 14.
24. Ibid., para 15.
25. Dalton, *Tribal History*, p. 179.
26. T.N.N. Singhdeo, *Singhbhum, Seraikela and Kharsawan – Through the Ages*, (Calcutta, no date), p. 26.
27. Roughsedge to Metcalfe, para 9.
28. Ibid., paras. 10–11, 13.
29. Dalton, *Tribal History*, p. 180.
30. Roughsedge to Metcalfe, para 26.

31. Ibid., para 29.
32. Ibid., para 15, 29.
33. Ibid., para 17.
34. Ibid., para 18.
35. Ibid., para 19.
36. Ibid., para 21.
37. Ibid., para 17.
38. Ibid.
39. Roughsedge to Nicol, paras 3-8; Dalton, *Tribal History*, p. 181.
40. Roughsedge to Metcalfe, para 26.
41. Ibid., para 29.
42. Dalton, *Tribal History*, p. 180.
43. Ibid.
44. Ibid., para 18.
45. Ibid.; Tickell, 'Memoir', pp. 803–5.
46. This conformed to British policy of Divide and Rule.
47. See Generalizations.
48. In a different situation 'aboriginal tribes of India' were considered 'little higher than monkeys'. Hardiman, *The Coming of the Devi*, pp. 14–5.
49. The politics of civilizing the colonized has been elabroated by Skaria, *Hybrid Histories*, pp. 154-5, 192–9.
50. The process started in 1838 and continued through the land revenue settlements of 1854, 1867, 1895 and 1913. Sahu, *The Kolhan,* pp. 132-6 and the record of rights issued to a Manki and Munda.
51. Wilkinson to Tickell, 13 May 1837, para 40.
52. See Generalizations.
53. Wilkinson to Tickell, 13 May 1837, paras 10–4.
54. Ibid.
55. This becomes clear from a reading of the Land Revenue Administration Reports of Singhbhum during British rule.
56. The essential link between the scale of civilization to which the community belonged and the corpus of knowledge has been conceptualized in A.K.Sen, 'Contesting Marginalization: Colonial Representation of the Indigenes in the Great Rebellion of 1857-58', presented at the *International Conference on Contesting Identities: Tribes, Indigenous Peoples and Adivasis in Colonial and Postcolonial India*, organized by Department of History, Visva Bharati, Santiniketan, 26-27 November, 2005. This portion is developed from this essay.
57. Said elaborates this in his famous lines: 'Additionally, the imaginative examination of things Oriental was based more or less exclusively upon a sovereign Western consciousness out of whose unchallenged centrality an Oriental world emerged, first according to general ideas about who or what was Oriental, then according to a detailed logic governed not simply by

empirical reality but by a battery of desires, repressions, investments and projections.' Edward Said, *Orientalism*, Penguin Books, (1985), p. 8.

58. R. Guha, *History at the Limit of World-History,* Oxford University Press, (New Delhi, 2002), pp. 4–12.
59. Dalton, *Tribal History*, p. 178; B.H. Baden-Powell, *The Indian Village Community*, Cosmo Publications, (Delhi, 1972), p. 153.
60. We can appropriate these traces from a reading of Tickell's 'Memoir'.

5

Singhbhum 1927-30 and the Tour Diary of Ratneshvar Roy

We have so far seen that historicization of the Ho has been a rather testing task. The haziness prevailing over crucial areas of investigation due to the absence of primary and secondary data makes Singhbhum and the Ho virtually into a zone of ignorance. This inspired me to explore untapped source materials that could provide additional information. Fortunately, I was recently led into the unedited hand-written official Tour Diary of Ratneshvar Roy, a British-day sub-deputy collector.[1] This chapter projects the Diary as a viable source for studying the history of Singhbhum. It first reconstructs the biography of the author of this Diary to know the social and official ambience as making the mind of a colonial-day Indian administrator. The second studies the corpus to highlight its significance and collates details from other contemporary sources to historically situate and remove a want, which often colours such private sources. The study ends by summarizing the findings to argue its usefulness as a historical document.

THE AUTHOR—A BIOGRAPHICAL NOTE

This biographical note[2] does not merely try to know from whom the work has originated. We know that the reporting official was merely an informant who reported circumstances according to the direction of his superior. Notwithstanding this limit in the authorship we cannot deny that what Ratneshvar reported was often a representation of his own understanding of the situation. This understanding was a construct of the socio-economic locus of the man. As I address this I find that Ratneshvar belonged to a family, who had migrated to

Chaibasa from neighbouring Bankura district of Bengal. It means that he was both spatio-ethnically an outsider (*diku*), who had been circumstanced to inhabit a tribe-dominated land and later to intervene decisively in their lives.

Son of a government employee posted at Chaibasa, Ratneshvar was born here in 1883. After passing matriculation examination from Chaibasa Zilla School, he went to Calcutta for collegial education at the Ripon College. In Calcutta the nationalist movement might have influenced him. His later pro-people concerns might be linked to this influence. The predominant trait in him was however a sense of duty and loyalty to the British. This was because he was throughout in government service. After temporary assignment as a teacher in the local Zilla School and then as the Sub Inspector of the excise department, Ratneshvar charted his permanent official career as the warehouse clerk under Sambalpur Deputy Commissioner. Next he became *Kanungo* for district of Singhbhum. His next lift was to the post of the Assistant Kolhan Superintendent. The title of Rai Saheb was conferred on him on 1 January 1930 in recognition of his sincere and efficient services especially in the field of mining.[3]

TOUR DIARY: CORPUS AND SIGNIFICANCE

The Tour Diary[4] begins on 10 June 1927, the day Ratneshvar joined as the Assistant Kolhan Superintendent, and ends on 17 December 1930. This contains his daily repots about Kolhan, Porahat and Dhalbhum. These are more or less detailed, in some cases covering as many as six pages. Compared to the Deputy Commissioner's annual tour report or the Settlement Officer's report this Diary is more voluminous containing in all 173 hand-written pages.[5]

The British ruled this country with the help of records, reports and manuals. These relate not only the technologies of governance but also the imperial notion of fact as self-evident pertaining to a given society.[6] The Tour Diary is a dispersed, incoherent and piecemeal reporting about the reality as evident to an official. As such it may appear to be unsound as an historical source. So a researcher has invariably to play the hermeneutic act of ordering the disjointed elements to make it a coherent whole. When I do this I am impressed by the diversity and rich details in this Diary on questions related to land, mining, forest, the advent of outsiders, popular discontent and protest, administration of justice, working of the local administration and other facts. Not found in such generic reports as the General Administration Reports or Land Revenue Administration Reports or reports on mines and forests some of these details make this Tour Diary an inescapable repository of regional knowledge. But even this hermeneutic work cannot absolve this source of the charge of often providing mere 'cues' or leads to the past. To remove this want I seek next to contextualize and critique it in the light of contemporary documents. These significant details form the subject matter of the following submission.

LAND ACQUISITION, LAND ALIENATION AND PEASANT PROTEST

The problem related to land constitutes a major theme of the Diary. We find the British government locked between two horns of a dilemma—preventing land alienation and yet acquiring tribal land for development. Another source informs that there had been a steady growth of land market in the districts of Ranchi, Hazaribagh, Palamau and Manbhum where large swathes of land had passed from *Adivasis* to *dikus*.[7] It is well known that this was the major cause behind tribal unrest in the nineteenth century, a fact that the British never wanted to recur. Yet they had to acquire tribal land for developing the infrastructure and subsequently for mines and industries. General Acts like the Land Acquisition (Mines) Act, 1885 (Act XVIII of 1885) or Land Acquisition Act, 1894 (Act 1 of 1894) were invoked to legitimize land transfer. But the special nature of Chotanagpur prompted the British to frame the Chotanagpur Tenancy Act of 1908 to facilitate land acquisition. Clause 50.1 (a.b) of the Act empowered the Deputy Commissioner to acquire land for

> 'charitable, religious or educational purpose or for the purpose of manufacture or irrigation, or as building ground for any such purpose and for the purpose of mining or any other purpose on payment of reasonable compensation'.[8]

The Tour Diary relates[9] that companies and individuals acquired lands for mining and government agencies for building school, dispensary, pond and laying pipelines for water supply. The corporate beneficiaries were the Tata Iron & Steel Company, Indian Iron & Steel Company, Messrs Bird & Company, Visanji Umarshi Company,

Kasimbazar Clay Factory, Messrs Villiers & Company and Schroder Smidth & Company, besides several Marwari, Gujarati, Bengali, Parsi and other Indian entrepreneurs.

While we can find richer details about the miners from other sources[10], this Diary exalts itself for reasons more than one. It provides detailed information about the procedure of land acquisition, compensation, problem of land alienation and consequent peasant protest. The method of acquiring land was that the lessee had to apply for issuing prospecting licence by stating the reason and extent of land to be acquired for mining. After official enquiry the licence was issued. Next it was converted into a mining licence when minerals were found in marketable quantum.[11] We learn that generally lands were acquired after arriving at an agreement between the owner and the government in which the Manki and Munda played a crucial role.[12] The quantum of compensation was fixed at market rates and it was delivered generally to the landowner in the village itself. But if the receiver remained absent at the time of payment, he had to collect the amount from Chaibasa treasury.[13] Providing him with another land sometimes compensated the landowner.[14] Disputes often arose requiring official mediation to ease tension.[15] But when the effort failed the government did not flinch from clamping down section 50 of the CNT Act.[16]

Land acquisitions naturally caused land alienation. The seriousness of the problem can be amply adduced from two reportings. One notes 'It may be remembered that half of the cultivated lands of Kurta were acquired last year & the other half this year.'[17] Another reports

> 'In the villages like Karanjia every inch of land has been recorded in the name of one tenant or the other. So that there is no way for replacing the *raiyats* with a fresh land for the land lost by him. By the money compensation paid to him he cannot buy other lands because nobody sells his holdings in Kolhan.'[18]

The second quote indicates that the land alienation could not be mitigated through land compensation because free land was not easily available. So it generally caused depeasantization. It also led to migration of villagers as shown in the Diary. It informs, 'The tenants seeing that they cannot make new lands from the waste settled with them in Gundijora, took thika settlement of rice lands in Keonjhar State. They are now busy in harvesting this crop.'[19] The problem that the Diary broached was however very grave. From another historical document we learn that in Dhalbhum subdivision the Bengal Iron and Steel Co. got the lease of over 12,800 acres of land for 35 years with effect from 1908. The Cape Copper Company Limited was given lease of over 1,166 acres of land for 45 years commencing from 1905.[20]

Though land acquisition sometimes benefited local inhabitants through employment, supply of drinking water, education, medical aid and rail or road conveyance, land transfers in most cases changed ownership from the locals to the outsiders. *Adivasis* were virtually placed on the razor's edge. Land was the only source of livelihood for most of them. Yet the compensation amount was an inescapable allurement. In the name of mediation, village and *pir* heads as well as the like of Ratneshvar, created a pressure-situation for them. Moreover, the fear of the imposition of the CNT Act was always there. So when procurement of consent through 'mutual consultation' was enacted peasants had to capitulate.

It is true that Ratneshvar did not mention this politics of consent, but he was conscious of the dialectical situation. He relates that the occasion for conflict arose more in cases when landowner's consent was not procured through mutual consultation or peasants disagreed to a proposal. One such instance was the tension between Bagchi, Lahiri and Company and the villagers of Rajanka and Kondowa. Ratneshvar noted 'The fact is that the tenants' lands within Tata's leasehold were acquired u/s 50 C.T.A. against the will of the tenants.'[21] This resulted in popular resistance.

Resistance was not armed; it was staged through non-co-operation and disobedience. In the above case, the villagers refused to accept compensation amount and sowed crops on the disputed lands.[22] Other instance was that of Rando Ho who refused to part with his plot no. 228 to the Kasimbazar Clay Factory.[23] Similarly, the villagers of Chota Mahuldia objected to the surrender of additional lands to the above Company.[24] Though rare, direct resistance was also offered as was done by the *raiyats*, Munda and Manki of Mahuldia against the Kasimbazar concern.[25]

This mode of popular resistance recorded by the Tour Diary disputes the notion that armed resistance constituted the natural and typically tribal mode of protest and supports the idea that their modes of resistance were existentially constructed.[26] In Chotanagpur and elsewhere in India they took recourse to diverse modes of protest like refusal to render forced labour to their landlords or to launch attacks on them, send delegations to fight feudal exploitation or the government's *abkari* system, indulge in crop and *hat* loot and also selectively forge alliances with movements developed by outsiders, particularly the nationalist movement. [27] The instances of peasant resistance reported by Ratneshvar may not be many, as are in other official documents but these provided a glimpse of the tip of simmering popular discontent, the entire body of which remained hidden from our knowledge.

The government believed that land was acquired for promoting development. But the question is, was the local administration totally oblivious of popular distress? This Diary presents the voice of reason emanating from the Indian element in local administration, which created a minor but significant ripple. It may perhaps be an exaggeration to project it as a conflict between nationalist and imperialist perceptions but indubitably Ratneshvar's kin in the administration sometimes had reservations, though not always articulated, about the role of land acquisition in development and public welfare.

Generally speaking the like of Ratneshvar favoured industrialization and growth of mining. So he sought to conciliate Kondowa villagers not to disturb activities in the Tata's leasehold. Recommending the Kasimbazar Clay Factory to the Deputy Commissioner he said, 'It is in all respects desirable that this farm should be given ample and bigger field to work upon'.[28] But he was equally concerned about the plight of poor villagers.[29] So he wrote, 'By leasing out a land for mining purposes Government derives royalty and lessee derives immense profit but the poor tenant loses his only resource of livelihood.'[30] While this comment underlines bureaucratic humanitarianism it also indicates a rift in the Raj lute. The displeased superior reprimanded Ratneshvar with the words

> 'It is always a difficult question to what extent tenants' rights should be sacrificed to the twin goddesses—industrial expansion and increase of earth's capacity to feed more mouths. It involves the question of what is the object of progress and development a question hardly within the province of a District Officer to decide.'[31]

MINING

During the early part of their rule Singhbhum appeared to be an economic liability to the British.[32] But they later learnt that like Manbhum and Palamau, Singhbhum was also a 'highly mineralized zone'.[33] The Diary relates that iron ore, manganese, chromite, copper, limestone, soft stone etc. were found in large quantity. Individual and corporate prospecting and mining projects[34] gradually activated Singhbhum. But with the advent of *dikus* life in this otherwise quiet and peaceful area became more complicated and tense.

These mine owners were outsiders and ethnically different from the tribal inhabitants of Singhbhum. They also brought people from outside to look after the mines.[35] Moreover, some outsiders acted as subsidiary mining contractors.[36] Mining prompted the growth of such industries as the Tata Iron & Steel Company and the Indian Copper Corporation at Maubhandar.[37] These pumped in still greater number of outsiders, details about which have, however, to be collated from trans-Diary sources. Otherwise allergic to *diku* immigration, the British government encouraged it to further colonial interest. An official source reports, 'With the opening up of mines and industries some relaxation will have to be made in these rules so that development is not retarded by difficulty in obtaining labour.'[38] The attitude of the locals to this influx was rather ambivalent. Understandably they were unhappy with the land alienation. But the prospect of employment[39] in the several mines, and the Companies at Jamshedpur and Maubhandar somewhat softened their grievance.

The Diary provides interesting and unconventional details about the working of the mining world. For its mineral resources Singbhhum had become the cynosure. Several 'news mongers' acted as 'professional suppliers of information to mining concessionaires who either cheat them or sell them some useful information'.[40]

The practices and malpractices of the miners formed another important theme. Abundance of minerals did not mean availability of uniformly good quality of minerals at all the places. Minerals of forty-per cent purity were profitable. So the mine owners generally blended superior and inferior qualities to make the staff marketable.[41] After carrying the haul on bullock cart or lorry to be dumped at the railway yard the minerals were generally sent outside through the railways. We have the novel instance of Visanji Umarshi and Company, which constructed a tramline to send minerals from the pit of their Baljori mine to the rail yard. But mineral-laden trucks had to be pushed from behind instead of being driven by the locomotive engine. Moreover, ropeways were used as was done between Budaburu and Ajitiya.[42] There are also instances of transport contracts being given to others.[43] Granting a sub-lease to a farm or person was also practised.[44] But this was not legal.[45] Minerals thus excavated and collected were sent to the Indian Iron Steel and Company, Raniganj Paper Mills and the Balmer Lawrie Company.[46]

Fig. 5.1: Iron ore mining

The Assistant Kolhan Superintendent had particularly to oversee whether rules and regulations had been followed. The Diary reports the tendency among prospectors and miners to violate the official procedure. They did not clearly demarcate the lease area and begin mining work within one year of the granting of lease as was obligatory.[47] Moreover, they sometimes encroached into the lands of the Forest Department as well as other mine owners.[48] Law was also violated when prior sanction for extending mining work was not sought.[49] These facts clearly showed that delinquency was rampant and the administration had to be very vigilant.

Mining created scope for employment. Labour was cheap and labour-related problems were rare. So local inhabitants got jobs in the mines and related activities. The Diary refers to 13-15 labourers being engaged at K.C. Trivedi's mines for dressing minerals and 5 female and male labourers at Dugar's mines.[50] These scanty informations, however, do not clearly reveal the spurt of employment prospect as reported elsewhere.[51] Ratneshvar is also silent about the rate of wages, employer-labour relations etc. at the mines. But it significantly informs[52] us about work culture among labourers. We find the prevalence of alcoholism and absenting from work owing to Hindu and tribal festivals. We have also the rare instance of a railway strike affecting transport of minerals.[53]

LOCAL DISPUTES AND ADMINISTRATION OF JUSTICE

The Diary reports several local disputes leading to litigations. Mining disputes between mine owners and tenants[54], ownership of land and trees, the use of water resources as well as assault and murder were the issues involved. Out of these, land was the most contentious issue disturbing familial and social peace.[55] Many of these disputes led to criminal cases u/s 426 and 447 of Indian Penal Code.[56] Though *zamindar*-tenant disputes were not relevant for Kolhan tribals as it was a government estate, we have the instance of land dispute between villagers of Robkera, Hessabera as well as Harta and the thakur of Anandpur.[57] Similarly, we learn about strained communal relations over land between Ho and Tantis.[58]

Another bone of contention was the tree, which was both a source of earning and status. Trees provided fuel and wood for constructing houses; *kusum*, *asan* and plum trees harboured insects that produced lac. So tree-related disputes were common.[59] We also have instance of two villages fighting over the use of *Jahera*.[60] People were involved in criminal cases over the use of canal water and pond water[61] or over catching of fish.[62]

For the tribal parts of the district, particularly Kolhan, the British introduced a system of expeditious justice through local enquiry and delivering quick judgement. This summary trial system can be elaborated through an instance. In a case u/s 447 IPC, after local inspection in the presence of the complainant, accused and lawyers, Ratneshvar heard both the parties and the lawyers and then delivered his judgement.[63] In the event of disputes not being resolved locally the venue shifted to the sub-divisional court at Chaibasa.[64] The Diary is silent about the process of justice at this level. But papers preserved at the District Record Room, Chaibasa are eloquent about the number of cases referred and fought here.[65] Next higher court of appeal was the Additional District Judge's Court at Purulia. Ratneshvar had often to depose in several cases relating to Singhbhum. Moreover, he had also to appear at the sub-divisional court of Jamshedpur.[66]

The above facts signify that litigations were on the rise. Secondly, British judicial system had gradually become more popular among people, particularly the tribals, than their traditional Manki-Munda system.[67] Thirdly, incidence of conflicts among *dikus* and tribals perhaps tended to widen their existing differences further and lastly, gradual weakening of the community bonds among the tribe was clearly evident.

TRENDS OF DEFORESTATION AND CONFLICT OVER FOREST RIGHTS

Besides the famous Saranda jungle, a sizeable part of Singhbhum was forest-clad. This natural forest was denuded to spread government network and for industrial activities. People often indulged in deforestation for village-making and other existentialist purposes. Though Ratneshvar was not asked to precisely report about deforestation, instances of denuding reserved forests by villagers caught his attention. The Diary reports about two forest disputes at Sonua over alleged falling of trees in Porahat.[68] But perhaps the most revealing instance was the one shown by the village heads of Bila, Sonua and Regarbera. They ignored the official boundary and marked a line across the neighbouring reserved forests to include portions of it within their villages.[69] We also come across the interesting account of destruction of the reserved forests of the zamindar of Bandgaon by the villagers of Matloin, Bidri and Royali to extend the village area and reclaim forest land for cultivation.[70]

Though above disputes were resolved after official intervention, these amply show conflict over forest rights between the British and villagers. I would, however, invite attention to other sources to understand the seriousness of the crisis, particularly to those forest papers, which recorded peaceful mass petitioning against official regulations. The Mankis, Mundas and Ho tenants sent one such to the government in 1907-8 against the marking off of a certain area for inclusion in the protected forests.[71] Similarly, 'thousands of Hos' petitioned against the new grazing tax on animals in Kolhan imposed by the Notification of 24 March 1922.[72] The next was the violation of forest rules. This they did by causing 'injury' to the forests by fire and unauthorized felling or removal of forest produce and grazing.[73]

While the British policy in general was conservationist[74] trying to save the forests from both the 'wildness' of the *Adivasis* and avarice of outsiders, these instances amply bear out that the tribals of Singhbhum challenged it by asserting their customary right over the forests.[75] This created a dialectical situation, which is relevant even today.

THE COMMUNICATION SYSTEM

By the 1930s, railway and road communications mainly promoted British imperial and colonial interests. From the Diary it becomes clear that the promotion of goods traffic was considered more important compared to passenger traffic particularly in Kolhan to set a trend that nationalist government later pursued. Residents of Chaibasa had to move to either Chakradharpur, a distance of 25 km or to Rajkharsawan 16 km away, to avail of the opportunity.[76] Besides inconveniencing people it impeded development. This reality particularly struck Ratneshvar. He wrote that the only means of transport from Baraiburu to Tatiba, near Noamundi in the mineral rich belt of Kolhan, was either via road or BI Company's light rail service from Selai. Ratneshvar lamented, 'Therefore I think nobody used to take keen interest in opening the area.'[77] Here however the official appeared to favour the extension of the railways to promote colonial interests

Fig. 5.2: A path leading to a jungle

Metalled and gravel roads had been constructed by the British. But meagre and damaged roads made journey across the district a painful experience for a common man and often retarded official work. On more than one occasion, Ratneshvar had to either walk on foot, use horse or interrupt his local inspections.[78] He particularly reiterated the pitiable condition of Kolhan roads.[79] Ascribing the blame to government's departure from the traditional system, he wrote:

> 'This is because it is now a neglected road. Before the introduction of Cess Act in Kolhan, it was a Kolhan road and in excellent order because the tenants used to maintain it. Now since they are made to pay cess, they are not required to maintain roads which has led to condemnation of many important village roads.'[80]

The above comment may be commensurate with the contemporary procedure or due to the uprightness of the concerned officer. What is more relevant today is, however, that a subordinate official's report stirred the superior. The Deputy Commissioner promptly enquired 'K.S. (Kolhan Superintendent), what do you suggest for the road?'[81]

MISCELLANY

The Tour Diary broaches many other contemporary issues. The day Ratneshvar joined the present official assignment he had to visit Jagannathpur and Jaintgarh in Kolhan to ease communal tension.[82] Though he skipped details, that communal problem should reach a remote tribal dominated Kolhan, merits further study. The next issue was Municipal and District Board election at Chakradharpur.[83] We also learn about the District Board dispensary at Dumuria near Mosabani.[84] The information about the election and the nature of public life or about the state of health and hygiene are, however, very sketchy. About health and hygiene other sources related that Municipality or District Board-managed dispensaries at such places as Chaibasa, Ghatsila, Jagannathpur and Dumuria, which along with some private practitioners, provided medical facilities to local patients. Though incidence of fever, bowel complaints, cholera and small pox had been regularly reported in the contemporary official sources, the Diary only refereed to the solitary instance of an outbreak of small pox at Chingijhari which stopped work at chromite mines.[85]

The Diary is, however a little more informed about official preparations for 1931 census in Singhbhum. We learn that the district Sub-divisional Officer was also the district Census Officer. Census operations began with house numbering done through the Mankis, Mundas and supervisors. But about supervisors the Diary does not contain further details. The census process was explained to people by distributing forms containing instructions followed, practical demonstration of the procedures by them and finally official inspection was conducted whether the work had been properly done.[86]

CONCLUSION

As I introduce this Tour Diary to the English-knowing readers[87] I am not oblivious of its various 'indeterminacies' due to the piecemeal and made-to-order nature of this narrative. To supplement the structural inadequacy of this genre of source the daily narrations have thus been integrated into a single narrative under different sub themes. This framework has been contextualized to create the historical ambience and then externally critiqued by comparison with and succour from other sources. In this form this corpus study leads us into the multiple recreation of Singhbhum as a region. First, it is an administrative transformation from a rule by the local chieftains and the Hos[88] to that by the British. Secondly, it is the remaking of an economic region practising agriculture, shifting and settled, foraging and limited trade-commerce into the mining and commercial hub of the empire. Lastly, it registered a demographic change from being purely the habitat of the tribal and non-tribals to be one also of the *dikus* from all over the country.

Next begins the bunch of three essays, which studies the impact of internal and external dynamics on Ho society during the entire span of British rule that forced them to redefine themselves against their own community, government and societies living around them. The first of these relate the question of Ho gender.

NOTES

1. Krishnendu Roy, a young advocate at the District Bar, Chaibasa, first

informed me about this Diary. It was made available to me by P.K. Ray. The Diary is presently preserved by them. The former is the great grandson of Ratneshvar while the latter is his grandson.

2. An interview of P.K.Ray taken on 4 April 1995; Detailed list of Permanent Establishment, DC's Office, GD, RB, CN XIN, FN 24 of 1918; Ibid., DC's Office, GD, RB, CN XIII AR, FN.23 of 1900-1; Ratneshvar Roy's application to the Deputy Commissioner, Singhbhum, 13 May 1908, FL, DC's Office, Excise Department, CN V, FN.2, 1908-9.
3. During the investiture ceremony, the Governor of Bihar and Orissa said, "You have spent all your gazetted service in the district of Singhbhum, where in dealing with mining questions you have combined a thorough knowledge of the rules and regulations and of the geology of Singhbhum district with a practical knowledge of mineralogy. In a district with mineral resources as important as those of Singhbhum this special knowledge has been of invaluable assistance to successive Deputy Commissioners." Sanad to Babu Ratneshvar Roy, Sub Deputy Collector, Bihar and Orissa, by Viceroy and Governor General of India, New Delhi, 1 January 1930; Speech delivered by His Excellency the Governor on the occasion of investiture with the title of Rai Saheb at Darbar held at Ranchi on 6 September 1930. Bihar and Orissa Secretariat D.O. No. 2673, 2708 PR, Ranchi, 10 September 1930.
4. *Tour Diary* of Rai Saheb Ratneshvar Roy (henceforth *TD*).
5. GAR (Singhbhum) 1878-9, May 1879 (Typed report, title page, Collection and File No. missing), pp. 1-3; Tour Diary of the Settlement Officer, Porahat, FL, CN VII, FN 2 of 1905-6. The Deputy Commissioner's tour report contains barely a few pages mentioning the places visited, periods of stay and brief information about the work performed. The Settlement Officer's report is almost similarly structured but more detailed at some places. Moreover, the head of the district toured generally during winter. But Ratneshvar had to tour round the year. Within the span of about three and a half years he toured 277 days in all, roughly a quarter of the total period.
6. R.S. Smith, 'Rule-by-records and rule-by-reports: complementary aspects of the British imperial rule of law', *Contributions to Indian Sociology* (n.s.) 19, 1, (1985), pp. 154-176.
7. Mohapatra, 'Land and Credit Market in Chotanagpur, 1880-1950', pp. 163-173.
8. S.N. Datta, *Chotanagpur Tenancy Act* (Bengal Act VI of 1908), 1908, (Patna, 1962), p. 66.
9. TD, 24.9.27, 20.10.27, 22./25.11.27, 17.2.28, 13.5.28, 12.8.28, 30.9.28, 28.12.28, 20.1.29, 19.3.29, 24.4.29, 18.5.30.
10. One of them is LRAR for 1928-29, FL, D.C's Office, GD, RB, CN. XI, FN 19 of 1929.
11. TD, 14.1.30, 18.5.30, see also 23.10.27, 20.5.28, 9.12.28.

12. Ibid., 25.4.28, 21.1.29, 9.3.29, 17.6.29, 7.10.29. About acquiring land for Sonua Irrigation Project, Ratneshvar reported 'tenants have no objection to part with the lands on reasonable compensation'. Ibid., 10.6.27.
13. Ibid., 20/21.10.27, 11.12.27, 30.9.28, 25.3.29, 12.11.29, 20.12.29.
14. For lands acquired from the villages of Kurta, they were given lands in the village Gundijora protected forests. Ibid., 18.6.29.
15. Ibid., 24.9.27, 17.2.28, 25.4.28, 21.1.29. The reality of prevailing tension may further be known from the Village Papers of Tuckey Settlement.
16. Ibid., 17.2.28, 27.3.30. To quote'Messrs Bagchi Lahiri & Co. sub lessees of Tata's limestone lease at Rajanka & Kondowa reported that the tenants had encroached upon their acquired lands and had sown paddy & other crops there. I was asked by D.C. to enquire locally. I went to Rajanka this afternoon after office work. The Rajanka tenants have done nothing. It is the tenants of Kondowa Munda that have sown paddy over the bera lands & one *gora* land. Besides some tenants have sown Ramtila on some *gora* lands also. Paikrai Munda of Kondowa told me that tenants are certainly wrong in cultivating the lands and he will warn them not to do so in future. The tenants concerned did not turn up. This trouble (occurs) every year. The fact is that tenants (tenants') lands within Tata's leasehold were acquired u/s 50 CTA (Chotanagpur Tenancy Act) agst (against) the will of the tenants. When compensation was distributed, all the tenants and Mundas refused to accept the same. Mr. Scott even failed to persuade them to take payments. At last the monies were deposited in the Treasury in the names of difft. (different) claimants. Since then the Munda of Rajanka and his *raiyats* have withdrawn the amounts. I am told that the tenants of Kondowa and the Munda have not yet withdrawn the compn. (compensation). It is for this reason that they claim the lands occasionally.' Ibid., 24.9.27.
17. Ibid., 20.10.27. The case of Kurta perhaps marks the zenith of the alienation process and the consequent popular predicament. Ratneshvar reported to the Deputy Commissioner that some portion of this village was outside the mining lease of Jamda block 1 being acquired 'last year' the balance of the Kurta village was acquired 'this year'. After compensation was paid the tenants evacuated 155.30 acres of agricultural wastelands as per agreement. As a result 61 tenants, of whom 52 were Hos, had to suffer. Before acquisition the Deputy Commissioner had directed the District Forest Officer, Chaibasa division to give the Kurta villagers 145.30 acres of land from the Gundijora protected forest block no. 45. Ratneshvar reported that tenants of Kurta wanted land in Gundijora as they could reclaim forestlands without much difficulty. Acquisition of Land in Kurta village by Messrs T.I. Still Company, DC's Office, GD, RB, CN XII, FN 4 of 1927.
18. TD, 3.3.29.
19. Ibid., 20.10.27.

20. LRAR, 1917-8, DC's Office, GD, RB, CN XI Return, FN 2 of 1918, paras 15(VII), XXX.
21. TD, 24.9.27.
22. Ibid.
23. Ibid., 17.2.28.
24. Ratenshvar reported 'They have great objection to because if the lease is extended they will have to loose their paddy fields.' Ibid., 25.4.28.
25. The tenants of Mahuldia objected to the Kasimbazar Clay Factory's attempt to extend the work. The compensation offer seemed inadequate as they contended 'if their lands are gone, it will be very difficult for them to live.' Ibid., 27.3.30.
26. Skaria, *Hybrid Histories*, p. 273.
27. Hardiman, *The Coming of the Devi*, p. 70; S. Dasgupta, 'Adivasi Politics in Midnapur, c. 1760–1924', *Subaltern Studies IV*, OUP, (Delhi, 1990), (1985), pp. 123-4 and T. Sarkar, 'Jitu Santal's Movement in Malda, 1924-1932', Ibid., p. 137.
28. TD, 25.4.28.
29. Ibid., 27.3.30. See also 17.5.30.
30. Ibid., 3.3.29.
31. Ibid.
32. They were dependent largely on inconsiderable land revenue collections.
33. LRAR, 1917-8, para 50.
34. TD, 24.9.27, 20.10.27, 20.11.27, 13.2.28, 16/25.4.28, 12.8.28.
35. Ibid., 20.10.27, 13.2.28, 14.1.30.
36. Ibid., 29.6.28, 4.6.30.
37. Ibid., 23.11.27, 2.8.28, 26.12.28.
38. LRAR, 1910-1, DC's Office, GD, RB, CN XIR, FN 12 of 1909-10, para 48.
39. Quantifying the number of jobs created requires an independent study.
40. TD, 19/30.4.29.
41. Ibid., 1/16.4.28, 27.5.28, 9.12.28, 12.8.28.
42. Ibid., 31.12. 27, 2/7/12.8.28.
43. Ibid., 13.2.28, See also 29.6.28.
44. Ibid., 24.9.27.
45. Ibid., 1.4.28.
46. Ibid., 6/16. 4.28, 12.8.28, 3.3.29.
47. Ibid., 20.11.27, 1.4.28, See also 9.3.29.
48. Ibid., 25.11.27, 11.8.28, 20.9.28, 25.3.29, 29.4.30.
49. Ibid., 20.9.28.
50. Ibid., 13.2.28.
51. LRAR 1913-4, DC's Office, GD, RB, CN XI, FN 1 of 1913-4 para 49; LRAR 1914-5, CN XIR, FN 8 of 1914-5, paras LXIX, L.

52. TD, 16.4.28, 27.3.29.
53. Ibid., 29.6.28.
54. Ibid., 24.9.27, 7.8.28, 27.3.29.
55. Ibid., 14/29.6.29, 19/21.7.29, 3/7.8.29, 21.9.29, 8.12.29, 16.5.30, 21.9.30.
56. Ibid., 21.8.27, 14.9.27, 16.10.27, 19.8.28.
57. Ibid., 7.12.27.
58. Ibid., 15.7.28.
59. Ibid., 2.3.29, 15/19/21.4.29, 16.5.29, 30.6.29, 31.7.29, 21.8.29, 11.1.30, 26.3.30, 28.6.30.
60. Ibid., 3/4.7.29. That *Jahera* became a bone of contention is significant area of study for the formulation of tribal religious belief.
61. Ibid., 7.9.27, 11.11.27, 3/4.7.29.
62. Ibid., 18.11.27, 25.5.30.
63. Ibid., 24.8.27. In a Kolhan appeal case, being directed by the Deputy Commissioner, Ratneshvar took the amin to Churgui village and after the demarcation of the disputed plot he assigned the ownership of the plot and four trees to Nandu Ho. Ibid., 10.05.28. See also 26.9.27, 25/26/30.3.30, 3/23.4.30. 16.5.30.
64. Ibid., 21.5.29.
65. Registers of Criminal Cases and Cravan and Tuckey Settlement Village Paper.
66. TD, 26/29.7.28, 20/21.8.28, 23-6.9.28., 16.9.29., 26.12.29.
67. When the Manki failed to effect partition between Madhua Ho and his father Jena Ho as per court orders Ratneshvar had personally to go and divide the disputed land and the trees to the satisfaction of both the parties. Ibid., 21.7.29.
68. Ibid., 6/20.11.27.
69. Ibid., 21.11.28.
70. Ibid., 8.11.28.
71. Formation of the Kolhan Protected Forest Block, FL., DC's Office, GD, RB, CN II, Forests, FN 9 of 1907-8, FS, 9. The problem of forest as both a cultural and contested zone see my paper 'Indigenous and Colonial Environmental Legacies-Collaboration and Conflict: The Ho of Kolhan during 1700-1918'.
72. Rules for Pasturage of cattle in Government protected Forests, FL, DC's Offices, GD, RB, CN II, FN 16 of 1923 and 5 of 1924, FS 24.
73. Forest Administration Report 1915-16, FL of English Correspondence, DC's Office, GD, RB, CN II, Forests, FN 9 of 1916 para 27.
74. Skaria, *Hybrid Histories*, pp. 199–204.
75. To understand this conflicting situation see A.K.Sen, 'Protected Forest Rules and Ho Social Protest, vide C.K. Paty (ed.), *Forest, Government and Tribe*, Concept Publishing Company Pvt. Ltd., (New Delhi, 2006): 78–88; R. Samaddar, *Memory, Identify, Power: Politics in the Jungle Mahals* (*West Bengal*), 1890-1950, Sangam Books, (London, 1998), p. 73.

76. TD, 20.10.27, 25/29.7.28. 19/21.8.28, 18/22.10.29
77. Ibid., 16.4.28.
78. Ibid., 19.4.29.
79. Ibid., 3/7.8.29, 21.9.29, 10.11.29, 29.4.30, 16.5.30.
80. Ibid., 16.5.30. The Cess Act was extended to Kolhan in 1917.
81. Ibid.
82. Ibid., 10.6.27.
83. Ibid., 25.8.27, 15/16.11.29, 17.10.30.
84. Ibid., 20.12.29.
85. Ibid., 10.1.29.
86. Ibid., 1/2/6/13.12.30.
87. A Bengali version entitled 'Raisaheb Ratneshvar Rayer Sarkari Safarnama O Singhbhum, 1927-30' was published in *Aitihasik*, Vol. 5. No. 1, Kartik-Chaitra, 1402 BS, pp. 75-88.
88. Porahat, Seraikela, Kharsawan and Dhalbhum were under the local chiefs, while the Hos dominated over Kolhan.

6

Articulating Gender, Social Response and Changing Ho Society

Tribal gender continues to be a rather under-worked area of scholarly engagement. In the generic texts[1] information about the gender is fragmentary because of the erasure of women in the sources they largely draw on.[2] This knowledge-blank epistemically marginalized tribal women and created the impression that they were invariably burdened and voiceless.[3] The other genre is the study of such select issues as property right to women and witchcraft.[4] According gender property right[5] had in recent times stoked Ho social protest through press, meetings and demonstrations. They criticized the attempted empowerment as a conspiracy hatched by *dikus* to destabilize their social order. While these undoubtedly touch upon two major areas of gender disempowerment, attempts to study select areas on the one hand make the intervention rather piecemeal and on the other somewhat diffuse the autonomy of the gender question by such issues as *diku* problem and witch murder.[6]

Against this grain this chapter largely draws on strategic Village Papers to argue that the abundance of information should merit tribal gender question more involved attention of researchers. Contextualizing Ho tribe of erstwhile Singhbhum, the chapter first seeks to approximate the position of women during pre-colonial times. Gender assertion due to the changed cultural context under British rule forms the subject matter of the second section. The third appropriates the actual rights conceded to Ho women, while the last relates areas of lingering powerlessness.

PRE-COLONIAL HO SOCIETY AND WOMEN

The dearth of oral evidence on Ho society compels us to depend on the codes of social institutions surviving up to British period to appropriate what might have been the original Ho order. Kolarian society, to which the Ho belonged, was originally matriarchal from which at an unknown past it had entered the age of patriarchy. At the time of Munda immigration into Singhbhum we find them rooted in the norms of patriarchal family, *killi* and village.[7]

We can form tentative knowledge of Ho women during pre-colonial period from early British ethnography. In 1840, Tickell observed 'no more restraint is placed on females than in our own society.'[8] One can presume that the community had not confined the women within four walls of the house. Instead they were allowed a full outdoor life, which 'their full share of labour in the fields'[9] proved. Moreover that at the family level women held a position of status and role in familial decision-making may be proved by two ethnographic observations. One related:

> 'The female sex, it may be observed, is not kept secluded and shut up, as is the case with the Hindoos and Mussulmans; they mingle freely with the men, even join them in council. The Coles are said to behave in a very kind and affectionate manner to their wives and female children.'[10]

The other informed that 'A Kol or Ho makes a regular companion of his wife. She is consulted in all difficulties and receives the fullest consideration due to her sex.'[11]

These proved that Ho society was then at a malleable patriarchal stage caused by different factors. Constant displacement and migration, the long power struggles between the Hos and others i.e. Bhuiyans, Saraks and Porahat *rajas* as well as anti-British struggles (1820-21, 1836-37, 1857-58), when womenfolk sustained men during the prolonged period of trauma and uncertainty, did not allow male chauvinism to ossify. Moreover, the collection of family necessities from forest and management of families as well as brunt of agriculture being carried out by women caused male dependence on the other sex for the management of economy also. In fact due to this larger share of women in material life[12] Ho men were not only characterized as 'henpecked' but also lethargic and indolent, vis-à-vis smart and energetic women.[13]

One can understand that Ho marriage customs were at once the cause and consequence of this gender position. The absence of child marriage and male polygamy helped in promoting healthy and less constricted growth of women.[14] The practice of widow marriage saved them from a degraded social position seen elsewhere. Moreover, unwedded state did not bring any disrepute to them, which the presence of a large number of aged spinsters showed.[15] Coupled with these the system of paying *gonong* to their guardians did not make daughters economic liabilities. Before British rule, not only in solemnization but also in the consummation of a marriage bride's family enjoyed an advantage. This they often applied by not sending their daughters to their husbands' house even after the exchange of bride-price.[16]

The above empowerment of Ho women was however accompanied by their perceptible deprivation in both material and ritual spheres. These restrictions seemed to have been coeval with Ho society's passage from matriarchy to patriarchy. First was the taboo against the use of bow and arrow by women.[17] Second was the restriction against gender use of plough.[18] Third and perhaps the most debilitating was denial of property right to women. Here we have largely rather solely to depend on Dalton for the original Ho custom. But before placing his point it is necessary to state that his information conflicted with the situation, which we find a few decades later. However, the lack of contrary cotemporary evidence forces us to use it axiomatically. Dalton wrote:

> 'An equal division of property amongst the sons appears to be the prevailing custom of inheritance, but they live together as an individual family until the youngest boy attains his majority, when the division is made. The sisters are regarded as livestock and allotted to the brothers just as are the cattle. Thus, if a man dies, leaving three sons, three daughters and thirty head of cattle, on a division each son would get ten head of cattle and one sister, but if there be only one sister they wait till she marries and divide the pan.'[19]

It is a categorical statement on the patrilineal custom and even denial of gender usufruct. It meant that on the death of father a daughter was to be maintained by her brother and in his absence by uncle who later became the owner of family property. Animal equivalence of gender perhaps suggests Dalton's mental lack when he had information, courtesy Dr. Hayes, of a high gender position in family life.[20]

BRITISH RULE: CULTURAL CONTEXT AND GENDER POSITION

British rule in a large way remade the Ho society. Though some of the details are available elsewhere in this work[21] I recount the relevant information for the sake of readers' convenience. After the subjugation of Kolhan in 1837 the Hos were incorporated into a formal state system for the first time[22] governed by an exotic legal system in the form of Wilkinson's civil and criminal rules. Though the Civil Procedure Code never was enforced here the Criminal Procedure Code and other all-India Acts were subsequently introduced in Kolhan. As a clog of British state machinery Manki-Mundas aided the Deputy Commissioner and other officials to run what was locally known as Kolhan system.[23] Indigenous method of controlling land by village community was virtually replaced when land became a property of the government. Communal ownership had to yield place to individual/familial right to property. The production process underwent major changes. From hunting, foraging and agriculture-dependent[24] pre-British mixed economy, agriculture grew to be the mainstay of their material life. Excavation of tanks both by the government and villagers and selective use of manure began in Kolhan.[25] It was gradually linked to market economy and the number of weekly markets grew over the years. We witness a gradual increase in the articles and volume of trade as well as participation of local *Adivasis* in market economy.

These factors combined to transform Kolhan society in a number of ways. First, the state system displaced village community as the repository and wielder of power. Secondly, concept of social equality, which only meant equality among the Hos within the superior position both of the *khuntkatti* family and *killi*[26], had to yield place to legal equality. Legal contract instead of social approval inducted literate culture in place of orality. These sapped tribal homogeneity built around *killi* and *hatu*. Lastly, with individuation of a Ho clamour for land increased both among men and women inspiring them to take more to British laws and courts to protect their rights. This undermined the importance of customs and village councils in Ho life.

These historical forces also influenced Ho women's life

profoundly. The most crucial was the extension of property right to daughters and widows.[27] We can cite some instances of registration in Ho women's names during Tuckey Settlement (1913): Joga Kui and Daskir Kui 130 *bigha* 13 *katha* 3 *dhur*[28], Sunai Kui 105-14-6[29], Jambi Kui widow of Buisa Ho 94-4-19[30] and Sunu Kui 60-8-5.[31] However, marginalization of women continued. One reason was the departure from the norm of monogamy to polygamy.[32] We notice that by the 1930s this anomaly had made deep inroads. Though often the trend was to marry sisters, which supposedly made a happy home of step wives[33], undermining of gender marital status obviously occurred when both love and control of family were shared. I shall later show that fear of husband bringing another woman, maltreatment of wives, neglect of children and strained relations between sisters and sisters-in-law became a nagging social problem. The other factor was the deterioration of economic condition of Ho families. First reason for deterioration was the progressive shrinkage of landed property due to partition. Second was that forest policy of reservation and protection stopped further colonization of forest areas, denying the society of the earlier unbridled opportunity of adding new territory to family's wealth by clearing forests.[34] So it may be argued that due to economic crisis, more particularly in poorer families, women became a liability, whose position in the family was commensurate with the labour performed for the upkeep of household and earning bread as wage labour. Moreover, there occurred disrhythming of traditional sex relations noted above adding to the vulnerability of women particularly in ordinary families. In this changed social milieu what we notice is the emergence of women as a subject with a consciousness of their social marginalization and a will to assert against the same. Gender articulation had several manifestations.

This was visible in the attempt to redefine marriage institution itself. We witness *apartipi* and *rajkhusi* forms of love marriage becoming more popular to socially settled *andar* marriage. Like the Munda and Santal, the Ho also solemnized marriage by paying *gonong* to bride's family.[35] When the rate of *gonong* rose and marriage in the normal way became difficult liaisons increased. To combat this evil social elders tried in 1868 and 1924 to reduce the rate and fix variable rates considering economic condition of families.[36] When these failed younger generation seemed to take recourse to love marriages ignoring settled marriage. This may be understood as a challenge offered by young men and women to the control of elders. Women violated marriage norms in other ways also. Though instances of such violation were not many, process of departure had started in Ho life. On the death of husband custom was to marry the widow with younger brother of the deceased. Custom was broken when Madai Kui married a person of her choice.[37] We have other instances of widows applying similar discretions.[38]

Ho society was known for 'proverbial fidelity' of women.[39] Departure from this norm was visible from early twentieth century though the process might have begun earlier. We learn of women of 'bad' character and ladies leading promiscuous lives.[40] Female promiscuity may be interpreted as gender protest against distortion of monogamous norm by men. We have learnt that even after marriage parents did not often send their daughters to their husbands. This pre-British social problem was compounded when daughters themselves refused to consummate the marriage. Maki Kui made a glaring example. She was duly married after exchange of *gonong*. But even after social intervention she declined to go to her husband's house. This forced her husband to snap marital tie by claiming *gonong* back.[41] It may be supposed that return of *gonong*, which the aggrieved husband was claiming, was socially evolved solution to this recurring problem. Ho society had to evolve another custom being forced by an articulate gender. We have instance of a married lady eloping with her lover.[42] That the problem was more endemic becomes clear from the custom of return of the entire bride price to the ex-husband by the lover.[43]

The above instances amply showed that Ho women had become assertive and ceased to be shy and introvert as before.[44] Gender articulation was however more frequent and extensive in the clamour for specific property rights through court. One may question gender proactivity in this regard pointing to widespread illiteracy and lack of comprehension of legal niceties. It may be attributed to prompting/help by other members of the family or village, even by lawyers. Though from files of court cases it is not possible to distinguish subjectivity from instrumentality, what we notice is tremendous female presence in court premises as both complainant and defendant. Possibly women had information of their rights governed by courts. They might also have been emboldened by freedom to move in the village and beyond. So they did not flinch from fighting cases at village level. But to lodge a regular civil suit intervention of a tout and then a lawyer cannot be ruled out. We have an instance of a case filed by a relative indirectly helped a lady. Birsa Ho petitioned the court for allowing him share in the property of his deceased relative Pasing Ho. On his death Birsa's other brothers had divided Pasing's land among themselves ignoring supposed claim of Birsa and decided to maintain Pasing's daughter Sini. When Birsa filed the suit the *panch* and court passed order to register the lands in Sini's name.[45] One may doubt, but for this intervention, the lady might have accepted the family arrangement of her being maintained by relatives without allotment of her share.

Instances of female initiative were also there. Fourteen ladies belonging to the family of late Sidu Manki of Choya, a *lakhiraj* village, claimed maintenance from government, as there was no male heir in the family. Since Kolhan courts had legalized right to maintenance, claiming the right to be allotted their share of land perhaps required no prompting. But interesting fact was that soon these women staked a claim over the entire village.[46] This claim was significant variously. First through this they were laying a claim for the Mundaship also, which was till then socially and juridically a male preserve.[47] Moreover, claim over the entire village had ceased to become a custom, which at the time of village making devolved on the family of the village founder. Since the idea of *lakhiraj* was a British innovation and registered a marginal place in Kolhan life specific knowledge about the institution was not social. So in the second part of the case dictation of relatives, villagers and lawyers might have occurred.

Ho women were found keen to protect property from the infringement of indigenous and exotic elements. Budhni Kolhin filed a suit praying that her husband's land be restored to her from the illegal possession of his brother. She was supported by her other relatives and the court ordered restoration.[48] In another, Subani Kui claimed due compensation from the Bengal Timber Trading Company who had acquired her three plots.[49] Similarly, Jingi Kolhin filed a suit against the government claiming remission of rent of her *bera* land which had been acquired for the construction of a *bandh*.[50]

Gender articulation often tended to be trans-customary. In the first case we find married women seeking to continue their title over parental property when customarily they enjoyed usufruct till marriage or death.[51] In fact, property consciousness had become so intense that women denied even their marriage to continue possession over maintenance plots.[52] Then we have the instances of some staking the right to control and enjoy first husband's property even after marrying a second time as Chariba Kui did.[53]

Similarly right to alienate was not socially permitted both to a male or female. To quote:

> 'A Ho cannot dispose of his lands as he chooses. The land does not belong to him; it is hereditary, inalienable, and must descend to his sons and sons' son; and if a Ho has no direct male issue, the land goes to his brother, or next kin; and if no kith or kin to the village community represented by the Munda.'[54]

Against these women claimed the right to gift, mortgage and sell property under their possession. Jobona Kui sought permission to mutate her deceased father's property in the name of her sister Kadama's son.[55] Palo and her sisters petitioned the court for transfer of their parental property to a person of their choice.[56] While the first case committed the infringement of patrilineal norm, the other intended to advantage persons of the above ladies' choice by transgressing the custom of devolution to all male heirs.

Ho women were equally articulate in protecting their rights as wives. Ganor Kui claimed share of property from her husband as he had turned her out of his house.[57] Jema Kolhin filed an interesting case. Her lover had impregnated her but he had refused to marry her. So she claimed *khorposh* from him through court.[58] Besides above instances of gender articulation to protect conjugal and property rights we have the novel and rather rare example of a widow executing a will at the court. With the consent of her unmarried daughters and the village council, mother of Mani and Chupad Kui executed a will transferring her property to her married daughter Mani and her husband, on the condition that they would maintain her unmarried daughters. The will was duly registered.[59]

AREAS OF GENDER EMPOWERMENT

Facts stated above amply evidence gender consciousness of social deprivation that inspired them to assert definite rights. But the question is why should patriarchal society succumb to female articulation? It may be argued that Ho social solidarity was severely tested by such factors as long period of migrancy, conflict for power, male dependence on women to run the socio-economy and the tension due to gender demand for greater social space. We should also look into the community's emotional life for more precise understanding of the tribal situation. The clues for a future extensive investigation are first that on the occasion of childbirth society assigned such duties like arranging midwife or cooking food or washing the newborn[60] to husbands. Next mortgage papers show both husband and wife's concern for each other and children. Often lands were mortgaged by husbands to procure resource for propitiating *bongas* due to the illness of wife or children.[61] So society was keen to evolve its own mechanism[62] to rationalize the problem of dialectical sex relations.

In this conducive social situation the British legal system instrumented the legitimization of gender claim to certain rights. Often therefore both court and society acted in tandem within the shared realm of British legal system to filter and reformulate Ho customs. This British-filtered custom was gradually internalized by the community as its original custom forming the basis for subsequent claim and counter-claim for rights. At the same time possible social reprisal against deviant behaviour by castigating a renegade as a witch was controlled by local administration. The cumulative result of the above factors was innovative gender enfranchisement detailed below.

First area was marriage. We have seen that prohibitive bride price caused the rise in *apartipi* and *rajikhusi* marriages both in well-off and common families. This forced society to rationalize the rate of *gonong* through social conventions. It was lowered for common families and in *rajikhusi* form payment itself was waived.[63] Next, society approved a widow's right to deviate from the norm of marrying husband's younger brother by marrying a person of her choice. These validations allowed ladies an extended area of freedom in marriage.

Allowing property right to women was perhaps a more decisive change. To recapitulate, pre-British Ho custom was that they were being maintained by near relatives without specific allotment of land to them. Subsequently, women became legal and socially accepted owners of property in various forms. First was the allotment of land on the death of father to an unmarried daughter, as her own share of paternal property, along with her brother/brothers. The case between *Bir Singh and Ruria Ho* vs. *Chandra Mohan Ho* related that on the death of their father the brothers allotted four plots to their sister. This was upheld by court.[64] A daughter became sole owner of paternal property when she was the sole heiress of deceased father. So when

Rando Ho of Goira died his lands were recorded in the name of his unmarried daughter Jobona.[65] Similarly, when a husband died heirless the widow became the sole claimant as shown above. But when she had children a widow was entitled to a share of husband's property as maintenance plot. In the case between Kiti and Pargana Ho both the brothers laid a claim over their mother's land. Their claim was overruled and the court ordered, 'As in all such cases the plot will be recorded as being in possession of their mother.'[66]

We have proofs of empowerment beyond marriage also. As stated before this was done to help a woman rendered helpless due to the absence of a male member in the family. Helplessness originated due to the taboo against woman ploughing a land. To mitigate this society innovated the practice of inviting a male relative to do the work of tilling and looking after ladies. This was at the root of *gharjamai* system to grow in Ho society. This was addressed in the case between Tirbhun Ho and Ubga Ho. Ladura having no male heir invited his son-in-law Tirbhun to live with him and look after his cultivation. He looked after Ladura and performed his last rites. The *panchayat* comprising two Mankis and Mundas recommended Ladura's land being settled with Tirbhun. This *panch* award and also natural justice seemed to influence the judge. On 5 May 1914, W. Kelly ordered, 'I see no reason why Tirbhun should be deprived of the lands; he gave his ancestral holding and by a court of his own people was given these lands. I think his right is established, it would be extremely hard on him to turn him out now.'[67]

This system often instrumented the passage of property to a married daughter and her children. In another case after Rompa's death his lands were recorded in the name of his daughter Jema on the basis of the *panch* award given by Mankis and Mundas. Significantly, her right continued even after marriage. When Jema's relatives challenged her right before court the judge not only upheld her title but also ruled 'After Jema Kui her sons are legally entitled to the land'.[68] This exemplified social departure from the ideal of gender usufruct till marriage or death and court legalizing the change. The observation of the court in yet another case amply showed that society itself was seeking to evolve a parallel norm. To quote 'I am told that this practice of making a brother-in-law or son-in-law reside in the village of his wife is not uncommon and the lands settled with such persons go down to their heirs.'[69] In doing so Ho society was acting in tandem with the Santal society where entitlement of daughter's family even after marriage had become more popular.[70]

Fig. 6.1: Women selling handia

Fig. 6.2: Ho women planting trees

During British rule society conceded outdoor freedom to women largely because of economic reasons. Finding living difficult from meagre lands marginal families sought seasonal employment either in the village or neighbouring villages during agricultural seasons or in the mines, brick-kilns or in construction work in near about towns or such far off places as Calcutta. The daily wage of a female labour locally was 4 pice per day. This sum brought a great relief to these families when in 1883-4 rice on an average sold at about 32 seers per rupee at the local market.[71] Women also frequented weekly markets to sell agricultural and other products or buy family necessities. The movement away from home and village as well as money earned through labour added new strength to Ho women and increased family's dependence on them. With freedom to marry and major burden of family work shouldered by them, this emboldened them to take independent decisions in their personal lives. This considerably loosened male control over the female.

AREAS OF DEPRIVATION

We should not however think that women had a field day. The inventory of gender deprivation noted below necessitates such probings as: how conducive was the social situation? And next how active was the colonial government in effecting social reform through law and judiciary? Obviously, Ho society was left at a crossroad seeking to rationalize gender demand for greater space while maintaining male hold on such crucial areas as property and indigenous institutions of governance. This sharpened the conflict between social norm and practice. On the other hand, the colonial officials were also in a state of dilemma. While they had on the one hand to maintain the ideal of British legal system of equality and justice they could not afford to be proactive due to the fear of tribal ferment. So they took the middle course of responding selectively to a social demand as and when it arose. The result was that society and British courts remained merely limited modernizers, so far as gender empowerment was concerned, perpetuating areas of deprivation.

First was the prevalence of restrictive norms in inheritance of property. Both ideally and practically society followed the patrilineal norm. Accordingly, while sons were entitled to an equal share, daughters merely received maintenance plots to eke out a living, and that too limited by the custom of reversion to male heir. In his order of 24 November 1916 A.D. Tuckey ruled 'The Hos give land in Khorposh to unmarried sister which reverts to the family on the girl's marriage or death.'[72] The governing idea was that sons were the rightful heirs and daughters' usufruct caused temporary suspension of their inheritance, to be reverted to them as and when sisters were either married or dead. In the case of Murum Ho and Gono Ho vrs Pasing Ho the court specifically ruled 'It is also the custom that all the land given to a sister are treated as joint property of all the brothers.'[73] On her marrying again the widow lost her ownership of first husband's property.[74] It may be reminded that even this right of usufruct was limited by the prohibition on women of using the plough necessitating male help for living.

Several forms of neglect of women as daughter or wife were practised. Budhni Kui filed a case against her father Hurdub claiming maintenance from him with the complaint that her stepmother ill-treated her.[75] Another example was that of Kel Kandu Ho demanding maintenance for him and his mother from his father Samu who after second marriage had driven both of them out of the house.[76] Ganor Kui lodged a complaint against her husband Tani claiming a share in his property as he had forced her out of his house.[77] But if we read Suru Kui's petition the predicament of Ho women would become very evident. Suru observed:

> 'I complain against Dising Ho of Tentera. I was married to him year before last. A daughter was born to me, but (she) died because he did not give me sufficient to eat. This is all I have against him. He does not beat me. He has no other wife.'[78]

This shows that conjugal life of a Ho woman was often threatened by three factors: denial of sufficient food i.e. bare survivalist needs, physical assault and bringing a second wife.

In the above case after court intervention Dising signed a written document agreeing to maintain his wife and daughter. So here British court system proved ameliorative. This was the reason why people often resorted to the exotic mode of relief rather than seeking redressal at village councils. But resorting to British courts was not very easy. It was a strange world where unfamiliar English and Hindi languages were in use; cases had to be lodged in writing instead of Ho verbal practice; procedural niceties had to be observed and considerable expenses incurred. Even then situation forced women to take recourse to regular civil court at Chaibasa.

Another area of denial was the disproportionate burden of familial work which hardly allowed Ho women much leisure. This becomes evident from the following social delineation of workspaces of sexes. The division of labour was not equal as revealed by the following quote[79]:

> 'In practice, the Ho men enjoy more leisure than women, and one is tempted to call them idlers. The women toil from morning to night, gather fuel, clean the house, collect Mohua, and other forest produce, go to the market or distant *hat* (italics mine) for sale or barter, wash clothes, prepare *Illi*, carry loads, work for wages in the urban areas and on return fulfill all the maternal and domestic obligations'.

Worst perhaps was social expectation from women non-fulfilment of which meant a social offence. To quote again 'Where women are not toilers and bread winners, they are ridiculed, regarded as anti-social, and even witches.'[80]

Tribal tradition of excluding women from collective decision-making woman[81] computed the helplessness of women. A Ho lady was not entitled to be either a Manki or Munda. Even though devolution of these posts followed the custom of property inheritance, She, who could partially or fully own father or husband's property, could in no case succeed to these posts. British government was instrumental in reinforcing Ho custom by inserting a clause in Manki and Munda's *patta* legalizing gender exclusion from these posts.[82] Similarly, the tradition of exclusive male composition of village *panchayats* continued. Not mundane but metaphysical world of *Deuri* was a male preserve. The last deprivation seems irksome when we have the instance of deceased *Deuri* Gola's wife to perhaps show the illogicality of the tradition. As *Deuri*'s wife she had full knowledge about all the functions attached to the office. When her husband died she trained her minor son for the post. But her talent did not earn her the office because society clung to the ideal of male succession.[83] Above deprivation left women no position to influence social decisions in their favour forcing them to follow male leadership in collective life.

CONCLUSION

Thus we notice a perceptible enfranchisement of Ho women. Their freedom in marriage, movement and selection of vocations were more or less socially conceded. Gender right to inherit entire or part of property largely during unmarried state and also selectively after marriage received both social and legal sanctions. The picture of an articulate gender marked a definite departure from its pre-British mores. Even though palpable areas of deprivation were socially retained, we have found Ho women resisting wrong done to them and fighting for their definite rights. This assertive gender, often aided by society and a responsive government, acted as an agent of historic change in Ho society.

This diachronic reading however stumbles before the contemporary reality presented by Kishwar. Her 'Toiling without Rights' creates an impression that there is hardly any articulation during the period of her fieldwork. Is it because of the failure of this study to be historically informed about the role of women in Ho life? Or is it due to growing male dominance over women, traces of which were visible during the period of this study, which had affected Ho society? Notwithstanding the reasons, the present account should enlighten researchers of the fact that present may be understood more thoroughly if informed by the past. But it is equally pertinent to note that the past can similarly be illuminated if we gradually regress, as Marc Bloch has suggested, through the terminal point of the present study to know how and where society or government has faltered. I now take up another area of transforming Ho society to critique the dominant diachronic as well as synchronic understanding of the Ho rather indigenous society in general.

NOTES

1. Roy, *The Mundas*, S.C. Roy, *Oraon Religion and Customs*, Edition Indian, 1972, (1928); Majumdar, *A Tribe in Transition*; Sahu, *The Kolhan*, pp. 202–3.
2. Tickell, 'Memoir on the Ho desum'; Dalton, *Tribal History;* Craven, *Final Report*; Tuckey, *Final Report.*
3. Majumdar, *A Tribe in Transition*, pp. 50–1; M. Kishwar, 'Toilng without Rights: Ho Women in Singhbhum', *Economic and Political Weekly*, 17, 24, 31 (January 1987).
4. Kishwar; 'Toilng without Rights'; G. Kelkar, & D. Nathan, 'Women's Land Rights and Witches', in M. Miri (ed.), *Continuity and Change in Tribal Society*. Indian Institute of Advanced Study, (Shimla, 1993); S. Bosu Mullick, 'Changes in Gender Relations and the Question of Witches' (Unpublished).

5. The backgound of the debate is that after the above empirical study, with another person Kishwar filed a civil suit at the Patna High Court claiming property right for Ho women. The majority judgment rejected the plea. But the dissentient judgment of Justice K. Ramaswamy observed that 'all forms of discrimination on grounds of gender is violative of fundamental freedoms and human rights. *Patna Law Journal Reports*, 1996 (2), October, Part 10, November, Part 11, Malhotra Books, (Patna, 1996), p. 134.
6. The general argument among the Hos, particularly men, has been that with gender property right tribal lands would pass to non-*Adivasis* who would seduce Ho ladies to marry them for lands. In this debate gender empowerment through property rights was subsumed by the lingering *diku* problem. Witch-killing, generally taken to be a law and order aberration, is also linked to question of ownership of landed property when the murder of unprotected women often takes place for the lure of land in her name.
7. Roy, *The Mundas',* pp. 229–30.
8. Tickell, 'Memoir', p. 784.
9. Dalton, *Tribal History*, p. 195.
10. W. Dunbar, 'Some Observations on the Manners, Customs, and Religious Opinions of the Lurka Coles'. *Journal of the Asiatic Society of Great Britain & Northern Ireland*, Vol. 18, 1861, p. 374.
11. Dalton, *Tribal History*, p. 194.
12. In economically backward families this activity seemed to be much larger when they had to perform 'the hardest duties in the fields, digging, shovelling, weeding, drawing water and getting food from the jungles.' Tickell, 'Memoir', p. 784.
13. Dalton, *Tribal History*, p. 194.
14. Marriage was performed only when 'both sexes attain(ed) puberty.' Moreover, the Hos 'restrict(ed) themselves to one wife.' Roughsedge to Metcalfe, 9 May 1820, No. 38, Extract Bengal Political Consultations, 3 June 1820, para 18
15. Dalton, *Tribal History*, p. 192.
16. This was listed as a major cause of dispute among Ho families in Kolhan.Wilkinson to Tickell, 13 May 1837, para 18.
17. It may be understood as the strategic disarming of women by men. But the traditionalists might argue that the restriction was imposed to save women from the hazards of frontal battles as they had always an indirect role during battles when they provided sustenance to male folk and accompanied them in the strategic retreat to the safety of hills and jungles during crisis.
18. In the dialectic analysis this may be taken as a male ploy to detach women from actual cultivation work. But again the conformists might argue that social prohibition was in fact a bid to save women from arduous tilling work. They might further reject the feminist charge by citing several crucial post-tilling works being assigned to women.
19. Dalton, *Tribal History*, pp. 201–2.
20. But one may yet argue that a Ho lady was not simply a liability. Besides

running family and economy, like cow she was an item of property because a father/brother/uncle could earn *gonong* through her.

21. See Chaps. II & VII.
22. A recent study however claims on the basis of inconclusive evidence that the Ho of Kolhan were incorporated earlier in the state system of Porahat Raj. Sanjukta Das Gupta, 'Rebellion in a Little Known District of the Empire', pp. 100–4.
23. Sen, *Wilkinson's Rules: Context, Content and Ramifications*, pp. vii-xx.
24. Peasantization of the Hos was differential. We learn of developed agriculture in northern Kolhan during the 1820s. Roughsedge to Metcalfe, 9 May 1820, para 17. But large areas of Kolhan had a backward techno-economy with lack of irrigation and manuring. Tickell, 'Memoir', pp. 804–5; Dunbar, 'Some Observations,' p. 372.
25. Craven, *Final Report*, pp. 6–13; See TSVN. I have elaborated the Ho method of the governance of water resources and the changes in their society in my unpublished paper 'Water Bodies, Changing Social Ecology and Ho Adivasis of Colonial Singhbhum'.
26. See The Process of Social Stratification for details.
27. However, this was not done through any regulation or legislation. In fact, Wilkinson's civil rules allowed Ho society to be governed by customs and customs at the time of framing of the rules in 1837 practised the maintenance of women by catering to their needs. Sen, *Wilkinson's Rules*, p. XVI.
28. TS, Papers of recordings u/s 85, p. 5, Jangiburu, VN 26.
29. Ibid., pp. 5–12, Bara Kaita, VN, 22.
30. Ibid., pp. 5–19, Pampara, VN 15.
31. Ibid., pp. 5–7, Tengrai, VN 14.
32. There is a strange coincidence between women's legal enfranchisement and social marginalisation. We can presume that trans-customary extension of property right to women destabilized male dominance. This was combated in a novel way by disenfranchising them socially through polygamy.
33. Majumdar, *A Tribe*, pp. 87–8.
34. I have elaborated the shrinkage of communal forest rights and emergent social protest in my unpublished essay 'Indigenous and Colonial Environmental Legacies—Collaboration and Conflict.' See also my essay 'Protected Forest Rules and Ho Social Protest', pp. 78–88.
35. The logic was to compensate loss of a working hand through marriage by payment of bride price.
36. Dalton, *Tribal History*, p. 192; Sahu, *The Kolhan*, p. 197.
37. TS, *Tanaza* papers of Karlajori, pp. 7–8, VN 63.
38. TS, Papers of cases u/s 83, p. 7, Abin, VN 6; TS, *Tanaza* papers of Saraqia, pp. 9–10, VN 42.
39. Tickell, 'Memoir', p. 807, Dalton, *Tribal History*, p. 192.
40. TS, *Tanaza* papers of Kumardungi, pp. 6–7, VN 33; Ibid., Kundubera, pp. 9–10, VN 55; TS, Miscellaneous Record, Chaibasa, p. 23, VN 62.

41. CS, FL, Misc. case no. 59 of 1908-9, FS 6, Tamalbandh, VN 103.
42. CS, FL, Misc. case no. 137 of 1908-9, pp. 1–6, Pukhariya, VN 284.
43. Dalton, *Tribal History*, p. 194.
44. Ibid., 206.
45. TS, *Tanaza* papers of Lupungutu, pp. 6–7, VN 62.
46. CS, FL, Mis Case No. 575 of 1907-8 of Choya, VN 2L.
47. In recent past we find some ladies being enfranchised as village heads.
48. CS, FL, Mis Case no. 162 of 1907-8, FS 11, pp. 2–3, Dopai, VN 14.
49. TS, *Tanaza* papers of Gomharia, pp. 13–4, VN 42.
50. CS, FL, Mis. Case no. 463 of 1903-4, pp. 2–5, Dopai, VN 14.
51. TS, *Tanaza* papers of Kumardungi, pp. 4–5, VN 33.
52. CS, FL, Mis case no.10 of 1908-9, pp. 2–14, FS 21, Goira, VN 139.
53. *TS, Tanaza* papers of Saradia, pp. 9–10, VN 42.
54. Craven, *Final Report,* p. 30.
55. CS, FL, Mis Case no. 10 of 1908-9, FS 21, pp. 2–14, Goira, VN 139.
56. CS, FL, Mis case no. 8 of 1909-10, Kear Chalan, VN, 38. See also CS, FL, Mis case no 42 of 1910-11, FS 6, pp. 1–4, Tholko, VN 51.
57. CS, FL, Mis case no 833 of 1909-10, FS 7, pp. 1–4, Hesabera, VN 232.
58. CS, FL, Mis case no 213 of 1911-12, FS 34, pp. 1–4, Goira, VN 139.
59. TS, *Tanaza* papers of Sarkand, pp. 4-5, VN 29.
60. Tickell, 'Memoir', p. 793; Majumdar, *A Tribe*, chaps. x–xi.
61. DR, FL 74 of 1909-10, FS 2-3, Kolhan Inspector's Report regarding transfers of land by sale, mortgage and ticca, Rajabassa, Kolhan, p. 21.
62. Two obvious instances may be provided. First was allowing usufruct to women to neutralize gender articulation. Next individual family's difficulty in cultivation due to the absence of male member was tackled by evolving *gharjamai* custom and as I shall show later in allowing property to be enjoyed and owned by married daughter's family.
63. Majumdar, *A Tribe*, pp. 98–100.
64. TS, Papers of cases u/s 83, p. 2, Pandrasali, VN 8.
65. CS, FL, Mis case no. 10 of 1908-9, p. 2, Goira, FS 21, VN 139.
66. TS, *Tanaza* papers of Khariaghar, pp. 17–8, VN 27.
67. TS, *Tanaza* papers of Bara Bankau, pp. 1–4, VN 3 of Chakradharpur thana.
68. Suit or Case no. 136 of 1906 in the Court of the Deputy Collector, p. 9. Serial 229 of 1906, Records of Kolhan Civil Suits and Appeals, Class I.
69. TS, *Tanaza* papers of Sidma, p. 13, VN 24.
70. W.G. Archer, *Tribal Law and Justice: A Report on the Santal*, Concept Publishing Company Pvt. Ltd., (New Delhi, 1984), pp. 40–1.
71. GAR 1883-4, p. 22, Appendix.
72. TS, Note for Orders by A. Tuckey, File A Misl. p. 10, Padampur, VN, 24.
73. TS, *Tanaza* papers of Suid Pokharia, pp. 7–8, VN, 54.
74. CS, Combined Title Page and Fly Leaf, Case no. 129 of 1914-15, pp. 1–3, FS 21, VN 175.
75. TS, *Tanaza* papers of Ruiya, pp. 29–30, VN, 42.

76. TS, Papers of cases u/s 83, pp. 3–4, Burumlata, VN 27.
77. CS, FL, Mis case no. 833 of 1909-10, pp. 1–4, Hesabera, VN 232.
78. CS, FL, Mis case no. 500 of 1909-10, pp. 2–5, Tentra, VN 242.
79. Majumdar, *A Tribe*, pp. 49–50.
80. Ibid., pp. 49–51.
81. P.O. Bodding, 'Some Remarks on the Position of Women among the Santals', in J. Troisi (ed), *The Santals: A Collection of Readings*, vol. 6, (New Delhi, 1979), p. 1.
82. This proves the point that the British in Kolhan was generally a forced modernizer.
83. TS, Papers of cases u/s 83, p. 7, Abin, VN 6.

7

The Process of Social Stratification in the Lineage Society of Kolhan

While studying the process of social stratification among the Ho, I have mainly to grapple with what is known as British ethnography and the knowledge created largely on its basis. This knowledge making being essentially utilitarian not only administratively necessary aspects of indigenous life was embodied but the same was also often uncritically repeated. The result was the structuration of an inadequate popular official literature. Drawing largely on the extant corpus later researches also suffered. This chapter purports to contextualize and critique the colonial picture of the Ho society of Chotanagpur by drawing upon a vast archive of district-level papers and documents. First, it examines British ethnographic and anthropological assumptions of a basically egalitarian and homogeneous Ho society and shows this to be a mis-reading of reality. Secondly, it probes the reasons why there was, in fact, socio-economic differentiation among the Hos. Lastly, it explores how the problem of the divergence between the historical and ethnographic-anthropological literature on the Hos developed during post-colonial decades.

THE NOTION OF A HOMOGENOUS AND EGALITARIAN TRIBAL SOCIETY

British ethnography does not provide us with exact information about the original Ho lineage system as it gradually evolved after the tribe migrated into Singhbhum. And we have hardly any oral information to help us. So an understanding of how the perception of the structure originally evolved has to be collaterally pieced together on the basis of official chronicles compiled from the 1820s. This ethnography generally sustains the notion of a homogenous and egalitarian Ho society.[1] Indeed, the theme of egalitarianism characterizes ethnography about Chotanagpur tribals in general. These sources insist that, except for minor differences between families, social stratification was absent in tribal society.[2] A recent study on Munda society ascribes this supposed equality to institutional control over village resources, shifting cultivation, inadequate artificial irrigation, mono cropping and the largely subsistence agrarian economy.[3]

With regard to the Hos, the common belief of imperial ethnographers was that they were able to maintain their pristine egalitarian social structure because of the geographical and cultural isolation of Singhbhum[4] from the stratified and non-egalitarian societies around them. But was this true? It cannot be denied that the lineage society of Singhbhum, and of Kolhan in particular, was less affected than that of the Chotanagpur plateau. Much before the advent of the British, the plateau areas saw a large-scale entry of outsiders.[5] But Singhbhum remained more or less free from this influx. So, when they initiated their offensive against the tribesmen of Singhbhum in 1820, the British found what they believed was an approximation of the original Ho social system (although subjected to the wear and tear of eight hundred years of evolution).

The notion of a 'levelled society'[6] seemed to the British to be sustained by the evidence of Ho socio-economy. When the tribesmen first entered Singhbhum, they had to clear jungles to found villages. Those who did so were known as *khuntkattidars*. Early immigrants gradually took to settled cultivation. But the Hos, particularly those who inhabited remote and forested areas, pursued shifting cultivation. We do not, however, have any information about the relative extent of shifting and settled cultivation.

The Ho economy was partially sustained by cocoon rearing, hunting and foraging, as well as by occasional raids (for loot) into adjacent areas.[7] But economic activity was geared to the domestic mode of production. Once the basic needs of the household had been met, the Hos saw no point in further labour.[8] Moreover, with the simple implements available to the Hos, who likewise lacked knowledge of irrigation or manuring[9], their agrarian society never generated a surplus sufficient to sustain an accumulation of capital. Village-based manufacturing and trade were carried on by people outside the community.[10] So the non-monetized Ho economy was incapable of generating enough of a marketable surplus to produce substantial economic growth, such as might lead to the enrichment of individuals.

The Ho social system was likewise infused with a strong communal bond. Collective affiliations to such institutions as family, *haga*, *killi* and *hatu* were emphasized while the spirit of individuality was discouraged.[11] Tribal solidarity was further perpetuated by the concept of property. We understand that land passed to sons as a rule, and in their absence to their nearest agnates. If no near relative existed, property passed to the village community headed by the Munda. Land could neither be mortgaged nor sold.[12] Thus we can conclude that land remained generally within the family, or was owned jointly by the community, precluding its concentration in the hands of ambitious and avaricious villagers. This way Ho lineage society developed an in-built mechanism, which effectively curbed the tendency to socio-economic differentiation.

State formation, with an accompanying process of Sanskritization, is generally held to be a factor in creating fissures in society.[13] But due to circumstances peculiar to itself, the Ho community could not reach the stage of state formation. To be sure the notion of kingship was not unknown to the people of the region. Kings had been a political factor in Kolhan, as related before, since the establishment of the Porahat raj in the thirteenth century. But the Hos had never fully recognized the claims of the Porahat dynasty. Although their relations with the *rajas* of Porahat were initially friendly, they gradually asserted their independence and except for paying an occasional *selamee*, refused to make regular payments to these chiefs.

Similarly, the Hos resisted the extension of Brahmanic values into their society through the agency of the Porahat *rajas*. They resented pilgrims to Jagannath (Puri) moving through their lands[14] to thwart the intrusion of any Hindu rather Brahmanic influence. The process of 'Rajputisation' identified as a catalyst for state formation and social stratification in the Chotanagpur plateau and elsewhere[15], was not thus allowed free play in Singhbhum.

The political organization of the pre-state Ho community also inhibited the creation of social cleavages. British ethnography tells us that the entire tribal-dominated parts of Singhbhum were loosely organized into a confederacy of *pirs* but without the notion of centralized government.[16] And any aggregate beyond the *pir* seems not to have evolved. Moreover, tribal society never evolved a mechanism for paying revenue to the Mundas or the Mankis. So village or *pir* heads could not replenish their coffers through taxation. The notion of a militia was also absent, though the tribal ethos sanctioned the possession of bows and arrows and battle-axes for offence and self-defence. And while every village had its *Deuri,* without a Manki-Munda-*Deuri* nexus, bestowal of ritual political status to village-*pir* heads does not seem to have been attempted. To sum up: without additional sources of income, military backing and ritual status, Manki-Munda headmen could not grow into overlords of the locality like their counterparts in the Chotanagpur plateau.[17] They remained merely social leaders, whom, as Roughsedge rightly observed, villagers 'obeyed more through prescriptions and attachment than fear'.[18]

FACTORS CONTRIBUTING TO SOCIO-ECONOMIC DIFFERENTIATION

We cannot, however, on the evidence of the above data, rule out the possibility that Ho society differentiated. As mentioned earlier, the collection of ethnographic and anthropological data during the colonial period was distorted by British 'desires, repressions...and prejudices'.[19] From the beginning, imperial ethnographers configured the Hos as the 'Other' of Indian civilization—not only geographically insulated from their neighbours, but also culturally separate from mainstream Hindu society. This became more intense after census operations began in the 1870s.[20] Moreover, the fixed and immutable image that featured in early colonial understanding of the Hos continued to colour the official vision of empirical reality even as new facts came to light, which challenged the stereotype.

However, by reading the colonial records against the grain, we can begin to reconstruct a more complex, and in some ways rather contrary, picture of pre-modern Ho society to that afforded by British ethnography per se. Let me begin this reconstruction by pointing to the factors, which may have set the ball of stratification rolling. One was the impact of ecology. Villages in the plains enjoyed an environment more favourable for cultivation than those in the hilly and forest areas of Kolhan. The state of having a more developed agriculture gave the people of the plains an economic edge over the people on the margins who practised shifting cultivation. Secondly, some tribesmen came into greater contact with more enterprising exotic elements, particularly the Brahmanic, which inspired in them a certain acquisitiveness lacking among those inhabiting the remote areas. Thus qualitative, and not infrequently quantitative, differences in landholding patterns, already evident as a result of village making, became more pronounced between clans of *khuntkatti* status and other *killi*s. Lastly, with the induction of exotic notions of kingship and feudalism through the agency of the local chiefs in and around Kolhan, inequality and heterogeneity seemed to have seeped into the tribal psyche particularly at the Manki-Munda level. Doubtless these factors were operative even during the pre-colonial period, but they proliferated in their impact during the colonial period.

After their conquest of the Ho territories in Singhbhum in 1837, the British undertook the task of 'civilising' the tribesmen of the region. This modernizing mission was carried out through land settlements, the introduction of a market economy, education and a western-style legal system. Soon the moral and material influences of these policies were affecting the very fabric of Ho society. Land settlements brought in the notion of family/individual property, which challenged the traditional system of communal ownership. Side by side with this, the introduction of mechanisms for the mortgaging and sale of lands converted land into a marketable unit and encouraged the more avaricious among the Hos to accumulate additional land. The multiplication of crops, the provision of greater access to markets, gradual contact with the outside world due to the introduction of railways and roads, the entry of outsiders and increased employment opportunities in mines and industries also brought major changes in Ho material life. Finally, the emergence of Mankis and Mundas as ground level functionaries of British imperial administration accentuated the process of stratification on the basis of wealth, caste and power.[21]

STRATA-MAKING IN HO LINEAGE SOCIETY

The paucity of both documentary and oral evidence precludes any attempt to elaborate the pre-British social scenario. Moreover, in the absence of data quantifying income in a predominantly agrarian society, an exact picture cannot be drawn for the British period. Even then a methodology may be proposed. These are the differential state of the village and *pir* heads, difference in land holdings and advantage provided by the privileged geographical situation. I now take up the play of these factors in creating and widening socio-economic wedges.

Let us examine the economic position of the village and *pir* heads first. We have a total of 68 Manki and 710 Munda families in 1866, which rose to 73 and 911 respectively in 1897.[22] They had various sources of earning. Mundas and Mankis were entitled respectively to 1/10th and 1/16th commissions of the total rent collected by them. The annual earning under this head was quantified as: Manki—Rs. 242-14 annas, Munda—Rs. 31-2-0.[23] Moreover, they also earned from lac and tassar reared by the villagers of the areas under their charge.[24] Some of them had yet the scope of acquiring ill-gotten wealth by settling *dikus* in their villages. These were besides their personal land holdings, which in several cases were larger than others. The following examples of the Mundas with the name of their villages and the quantum of land possessed by them will prove the point.[25]

Name	*Village*	*Size of landholding*
Binusingh Munda	Nawamundi	155 *bigha* 17 *katha* 19 *dhur*
Unu Munda	Kuchibera	109-11-6
Pradhan Munda & another	Uisia	174-19-18
Kainua Munda	Rengarbera	115-15-6
Jamadar Munda	Duarsai	189-19-3

Note: One *bigha* was less than one-third of an acre, a *katha* was about 80 sq. yards and a *dhur* was one-twentieth part of a *katha*.

If we compute the earning say of Binusingh from commission as Rs. 25-9-9 and Rs. 30-6-0 of Unu Munda their better state can be understood.[26] Yet they were not the richest of the Hos. Sadhu Manki of Khas Pukharia village and Banmali Manki of Asura were identified as the richest among the Hos, the former possessing wealth worth more than one lakh rupees.[27] As well, some Mankis, Mundas and substantial villagers (to be identified later) had the means to excavate tanks.[28] This fact is historically significant because about seven decades earlier Tickell had lamented the absence of resources among *raiyats* to finance such works.[29] Moreover, resourceful Mankis could take out leases on *bandhs* or on the Roro or Kharkai rivers for fishing.[30] These water resources provided irrigation facilities to their lands, enabling them to produce more crops and further raise their economic standard.

Another reason for the emergence of socio-economic heterogeneity among the Hos was the qualitative and quantitative differences in land possession. This standard may be studied at two levels. First we should note the distinction observed between *khuntkatti* and non-*khuntkatti* families, which privileged the former in many villages. In Barajaipur, for instance, out of a total of about 792 *bigha*s of arable land in the possession of 33 tenants, four *khuntkatti* families alone owned over 406 *bigha*s. This means that one-eighth of the village population possessed more than half of the total cultivable land.[31] In fact, when villages were founded in Kolhan the common trend was to allocate the best quality land to the families of the founding *killi*s. Clearly, *khuntkatti* status was the key to material advancement in Ho society.

Second, and more generally, we may note the distribution of land owning by individual families. The available data suggests a rarified social pyramid.[32] For instance in Bara Chiru, where there were in all 141 tenancies, the distribution was as follows: 16 holdings were less than one *bigha* in size; 91 were between one and ten *bigha*s; 26 were between ten and twenty *bigha*s; 1 was between twenty and thirty *bigha*s; and 2 were more than forty *bigha*s in area. This shows that the marginalized families, i.e. those owning ten or less *bigha*s, were in the overwhelming majority.[33] Likewise in Tantnagar village, only 5 of 53 landholders owned more than forty *bigha*s. Of these, 3 families possessed more than one hundred *bighas*.[34]

While the above picture helps us to understand strata formation at micro-village level, heterogeneity on a much broader scale emerges when data about the quality of land due to geographical location is used as a marker.[35] The southern part of Bar *pir* and the southwestern part of Aola *pir* were flat and open terrain, and the soil was richer there than elsewhere in Kolhan. On the other hand, the greater part of Asantalia, Ajudhia, Chainpur, Sidu, Lota, Rajabassa, Chiru, Cherai, much of Gumra and Bharbharia *pirs* and the eastern portion of Thai *pir* were also open but less fertile. All these *pir*s contained numerous prosperous and well-cultivated villages. Moreover, agricultural development here was substantially facilitated by irrigation works, over one-third of all rice lands in Ajudhia, Lota, Rajabassa and Asantalia *pir*s enjoying access to permanent water.[36] Many families residing in these *pir*s also started to make a good living by supplementing their earning from the cultivation of tassar cocoon and lac, especially from the 1860s.

On the other hand, eastern Aola, Lalgarh, south Nagra, Jamda, Rengra, Rela, Latua, Saranda, southern Kuldiha, Kainua, Golkera, the western parts of Barkela and Gumra and the northern parts of Bantaria and Kotegarh *pirs* were mountainous tracts covered with jungles. These physical disabilities, augmented by the comparative absence of irrigation in the highlands, retarded agricultural development. People of these areas were thus disadvantaged compared to the inhabitants of *pirs* in the plains. But within these *pirs*, too, economic disparities proliferated due to the varying fertility of the land.[37] One-third of rice-growing land in southern Kuldiha, Kainua and Golkera was irrigated, but only one-sixtieth in Lalgarh and even less in Rela, Nagra, Rengra, Latua and Saranda.[38] Yet the presence of a well-off stratum of cultivators in rural Kolhan is attested to by the fact that 661 private *bandhs* were constructed there in the late nineteenth century, irrigating ten per cent of the total cultivated area.[39]

To sum up, it may be said that the top rung of the Ho social ladder consisted of most of the families of Mankis, the majority of Munda families, and families with substantial land holdings, say those owning one hundred or more *bighas*. Families below this social level holding, say forty or more *bighas* land, might be placed in the middle category.

The question may be asked, though, whether socio-economic difference was otherwise visible. It was. One marker was the substantial and capacious residences of the village heads which, as early as the 1840s, had sleeping rooms, drawing rooms and storerooms, smaller constructions away from the main houses for servants or travellers, granaries, and buildings housing cows, pigs, and pigeons.[40] Another was the absence of debt among the Ho elite who, in contrast to other rural dwellers in this period, managed to subsist comfortably without the dubious aid of the moneylenders. Yet a third was the elites' possession of objects of utility and display. British observers noted that they were invariably well dressed. They used brass and metal utensils rather than earthen ones.[41] And they ate regularly twice a day—at noon and at night. A typical meal for one of these families included boiled rice, *dal* (pulse), and *sag*, supplemented by *handia*.[42]

At the base of the social ladder were families with meagre landholdings mostly situated in the jungle and hilly areas of Kolhan. These survived often by working part-time as menials in the households of Mankis, Mundas or other substantial *raiyats*[43], or as day labourers in the mines or on railway construction projects. As for the people of the dense jungle areas, they had to depend solely on rudimentary cultivation and jungle products. These tribals lived in rude huts[44], and partook of a frugal diet consisting in large part of *mahua* flowers, wild roots, fruits and leaves gathered in the jungle[45], sometimes supplemented by the flesh of wild pigs.[46] Their women wore no upper garments, merely a rag round their loins.[47]

Last but not least, evidence of stratification in Ho society can be gleaned from the decisions reached in 1868, and 1924 at meetings of tribal leaders to curb *gonong*. In 1868 the maximum rate of *gonong* was fixed at ten head of cattle or its equivalent (i.e. one pair of oxen, one cow and seven rupees). But for the poorer members of the tribe the rate was set at only seven rupees. Likewise in 1924, the rate was set at thirty rupees, two bullocks and a cow for those who possessed land, and only ten rupees for those who were landless.[48]

It may be pointed out that society was defining socio-economic hierarchies in unison with colonial state because the above meetings were convened under the aegis of local administration. Right from the time of Tickell to the end of colonial rule, British ethnographers could find that their policies had been changing the traditional socio-economic structure. Reared in a stratified society under a growing colonial industrial economy, to the British administrator-ethnographers in Kolhan the usher of socio-economic wedges perhaps seemed to be evident and perhaps provable markers of the material progress of the Hos, about which references profuse in their annual land revenue reports. So they believed, that consciously or unconsciously they had been able to project a new model of lineage structure, which could be effectively utilized for the common benefit of both the ruler and ruled. Mankis and Mundas were inducted to collect land revenue, and they along with substantial *raiyats* helped in administering justice. Moreover, these substantial families were emerging as a counterpoise to hereditary tribal leadership also. As a result, the traditional society was forced to provide space to them in the existing power structure. This was happening with the help of local administration who accommodated them in the village *panchayats* in administering justice.[49] At the sametime, the marginal peasants and landless formed the migrant labour force for collieries and tea gardens to serve colonial economy.[50]

The above empirical information on Ho social strata, collected largely from Village Papers, however failed to find place in more generic and easily available British reports and gazetteer.[51] When we reason the duality, we are led into the compulsions of a colonial knowledge-maker. First, he was providing the database to help administrators in framing policies and implementing them. But he had also to abide by the imperialist imperative of establishing the tribe as essentially different from the rest of Indians.

However, while accepting this politics in the colonial construction of knowledge one has also to accept that a relative reading of tribal and non-tribal societies revealed to them that hierarchies were not generally comparable with that found in non-tribal societies. Ethnographers could reason that phenomenal laziness, improvidence, absence of a desire for material promotion, easy availability of land and bias of the Hos for agriculture as against industrial work prevented the free play of critical forces in sharpening hierarchies.[52]

A closer reading of the historical situation would however have added some more factors. These were first that the basic agrarian structure continued without major change particularly in the use of modern technology. Secondly, concentration of land in a few hands was prevented by an alert local administration. Next, though mining and industrial activities began tribals could merely participate as unskilled workers there. Similarly in commercial sector the indigenous people remained confined to the role of mere grower and seller of primary products. For a Ho opting for a non-agrarian vocation of a miner, industrialist or a trader was hindered by an obvious lack of capital besides the cultural bias for agriculture stated above. Lastly, Mankis and Mundas could only perform a subordinate role in the existing power structure. So though socio-economic fissures had emerged, Ho society still presented a picture of contrast from the mainstream of Indian society.

CONTRASTING REALITIES: HISTORICAL PAST AND POST-COLONIAL ETHNOGRAPHY AND ANTHROPOLOGY

In this study I have projected two pictures during colonial period, one drawn by the ethnographers-anthropologists and the other by a researcher drawing mainly on more informed local resources. I have perhaps been able to show that the former barely dilated the reality of socio-economic disparities. This want is removed when Ho social history is appropriated from Village Papers. As I enter the domain of post-colonial official papers and anthropology I find the tradition of reticence lingering. The corpus of this knowledge found in the District Gazetteer and Settlement Report embody frail cultural inventory about the Hos. Of these two the Report suggests Ho society being divided into better off/wealthy and average/ poor, manifest in their distinct house structures and funeral practices.[53] On the other hand, the usual 'People' section of the Gazetteer, still partially depending for information on Tickell and Dalton, fails to provide even this detail on socio-economic hierarchies. It only mentions, like the above, about the cremation practice of rich families, thereby suggesting that the poor practised burial.[54]

The picture drawn by anthropologists is equally peripheral. About tribe in general and Indian tribes in particular the dominant idea is that of 'cultural homogeneity and cultural continuity'[55], 'segmentary system and absence of inequalities of class'[56] and 'non-hierarchic and undifferentiated' society.[57] In anthropology these are generally taken to be essential parameters for drawing boundaries between a tribe and non-tribe. Though essentialization of these parameters are increasingly more questioned, as in the texts cited above, an empirical work, when diachronically informed, tends to accept the notion of stratification.[58] Even then there is no marked change, as material evidences do not substantiate the idea. I would particularly refer an empirical work on Ho life itself. It also fails, like the general one on tribe stated above, to develop the distinctions between average families/lower sections of the tribe and Manki-Munda families/higher classes as well as substantial cultivators.[59] This failure may largely be ascribed to the lack of a diachronic reading of tribal societies. But the correction of this inadequacy is highly essential to be informed about another crucial historical phenomenon. The next chapter seeks precisely to explore this.

NOTES

1. Although Tickell, for example, sometimes employs contradictory expressions such as 'high' and 'low', and 'the better classes'. See Tickell, 'Memoir', pp. 783–4.
2. Roy, *The Mundas*, pp. 211–18; S.C. Roy, *The Oraons of Chotanagpur*, Man in India, (Ranchi, 1984), pp. 59–60; and Majumdar, *A Tribe in Transition*, pp. 26–7.
3. B.B. Chaudhuri, 'Tribal Society in Transition: Eastern India, 1757–1920', in M. Hasan and N. Gupta (eds), *India's Colonial Encounter: Essays in*

Honour of Eric Stokes, Manohar, (Delhi, 1993), pp. 68–76.

4. Bradley-Birt, *Chota Nagpore,* pp. 85–6; Tickell, 'Memoir', pp. 696–7; Dalton, *Tribal History*, pp. 177, 185; Roughsedge to Metcalfe, 9 May 1820, para 13.
5. K.S. Singh, *Birsa Munda and His Movement 1874-1901,* Oxford University Press, (Calcutta, 1983), pp. 9–17.
6. Tickell, 'Memoir', p. 804.
7. Tickell, 'Memoir', p. 805; and Tuckey, *Final Report*, p. 118.
8. E. Roughsedge to George Swinton, 14 April 1821, SWFPDR, 2 April 1821 to 10 Dec. 1821, Vol. XXIX, para 13.
9. Tickell, 'Memoir', pp. 804–5.
10. Roughsedge to Metcalfe, 9 May 1820, para 16; Tickell, 'Memoir', pp. 804–5; Dalton, *Tribal History*, p. 185.
11. Tickell, 'Memoir', p. 785; Craven, *Final Report*, pp. 19–20; Majumdar, *A Tribe in Transition*, pp. 55–9; Sahu, *The Kolhan*, pp. 170–2.
12. S.J. Manook to C.H. Bompas, dep. comm. Singhbhum, 3 Sept. 1895, appended to J.A. Craven to dep. comm. Singhbhum, 21 Aug. 1895; *vide* W.H. Grimley to sec. to Board of Revenue, Lower Provinces, no. 876LR, 14 Oct. 1895, RD, FN 16-S/2, nos. 113–4.
13. Sinha, 'State Formation and Rajput Myth', pp. 41–71.
14. Roughsedge to Metcalfe, 9 May 1820, para 13; Tickell, 'Memoir', p. 697.
15. Sinha, 'State Formation', pp. 36–71. Also see J.C. Jha, *The Tribal Revolt of Chotanagpur 1831-32,* K.P. Jayaswal Research Institute (Patna, 1987), pp. 130–1.
16. B.H. Baden-Powell, *The Indian Village Community*, Cosmo Publications, (Delhi, 1972), p. 153.
17. K.S. Singh, 'The Munda Land System and Revenue Reforms in Chotanagpur During 1869-1908', in R.S. Sharma (ed.), *Land Revenue in India: Historical Studies,* Motilal Banarsidass, (Patna, 1971), pp. 80–90.
18. Roughsedge to Metcalfe, 9 May 1820, para 19.
19. Said, *Orientalism*, p. 8.
20. A.K. Sen, 'Conceptualisation of the Hos of Singhbhum as a Tribe', in P. Sen (ed.), *Changing Tribal Life: A Socio-Philosophical Perspective*, Concept Publishing Company Pvt. Ltd., (New Delhi, 2003), pp. 1–14.
21. Craven, *Final Report*, pp. 124–5; Tuckey, *Final Report*, pp. 2–3, 118–9; O'Malley, *Bengal District Gazetteers*, pp. 117, 151 8; P.C. Roy Chaudhury, *Bihar District Gazetteers Singhbhum*, Superintendent, Secretariat Press, (Patna, 1958), pp. 112–4, 193–6, 343–6; Sahu, *The Kolhan*, pp. 218–22, 230–5, 238–9, 244.
22. Hunter, *SAB*, pp. 74-6; Craven, *Final Report*, p. 54.
23. Craven, *Final Report*, p. 54.
24. Tuckey, *Final Report*, p. 41; Sahu, *The Kolhan*, p. 139.
25. TS, Records of cases u/s 346/85 (2) ii of 1917, Duarsai, VN 70, pp. 5–10; Ibid., u/s 334/85 (2) ii of 1917, Rengarbera, VN 71, pp. 5–9; Ibid., u/s 333/

85 (2) ii of 1917, Uisia, VN 71, pp. 5–8; Ibid., u/s 332/85 (2) ii of 1917, Kuchibera, VN 71, pp. 5–7 Ibid., u/s 327/ 85 (2) ii of 1917, Nawamundi, VN 71, pp. 5–7.

26. Ibid., Kuchibera and Nawamundi.
27. Tuckey, *Final Report*, pp. 120–1.
28. TSVN, Khajuria and Khas Pukhuria, Vol. II, pp. 316, 396. Many other villagers owning tanks could also be cited from the above source.
29. Tickell, 'Memoir', p. 804.
30. TSVN, Vols. I & II.
31. TS, Records of Cases u/s 28/85 (2) ii of 1917, Barajaipur, VN 13, pp. 5–12. See also Ibid., Records of Cases u/s 368/85 (2) ii of 1917, Dumarjua, VN 68, pp. 5–13; and Records of Cases u/s 364/85 (2) ii of 1917, Kitaktorang, VN 68, pp. 5–10.
32. The projections are, however, a tentative identification of socio-economic layers as productivity and earning depended more on the quality of land as well as its geographical location. However, marginals and non-marginals may be identified clearly. Tickell observed a Ho 'worth three or four ploughs, lives in a very comfortable manner'. Tickell, 'Memoir', p. 783.
33. TS, Records of Cases u/s 685/85 (2) ii of 1917, Bara Chiru, VN 12, pp. 5–21. Another instance is Ibid., Record of Cases u/s 515/85 (2) ii of 1917, Tantnagar, VN 15, pp. 5–21.
34. Ibid., Records of Cases u/s 598/85 (2) ii of 1917, Tensera, VN 67, pp. 5–11. See also Ibid., Records of Cases u/s 604/85 (2) ii of 1917, Suiamba, VN 67, pp. 5–14.
35. Kolhan had three classes of land: *bera, bad* and *gora* having 76.2, 228.1 and 220.3 square miles in area respectively. Craven, *Final Report*, p. 23.
36. Ibid., p. 5; Tuckey, *Final Report*, p. 5.
37. Craven, *Final Report*, p. 2.
38. Ibid., Tuckey, *Final Report*, p. 5.
39. Craven, *Final Report*, pp. 24–5.
40. Tickell, 'Memoir', p. 783.
41. O'Malley, *Bengal District Gazetteers*, p. 134.
42. Craven, *Final Report*, p. 22.
43. These menials were paid poorly, and often in kind. Ibid., pp. 181–2; O'Malley, *Bengal District Gazetteers*, p. 133.
44. Bradley-Birt, *Chota Nagpore*, p. 87; Craven, *Final Report*, p. 2; Majumdar, *A Tribe in Transition*, pp. 17–9.
45. Craven, *Final Report*, p. 2.
46. Tickell, 'Memoir', p. 803; Dalton, *Tribal History*, p. 201.
47. Tickell, 'Memoir', p. 784.
48. Dalton, *Tribal History*, p. 192; Sahu, *The Kolhan*, pp. 197–8.
49. The entire issue of the role of village heads and of substantial *raiyats* is taken up in my unpublished monograph: *From Village Elder to British Judge: Custom, Customary Law and Tribal Society*.
50. For details see P.P. Mohapatra, 'Coolies and Colliers: A Study of the Agrarian

Context of Labour Migration from Chotanagpur, 1880-1920', *Studies in History*, 1, 2, n.s. (1985); and the next essay.

51. I have in mind Craven, *Final Report*; Tuckey, *Final Report;* O'Malley, *Bengal District Gazetteer*.
52. Craven, *Final Report*, p. 22; Tuckey, *Final Report*, p. 10; O' Malley, *Bengal District Gazetteers*, pp. 133, 136. We know that the image of a lazy, easy-going and improvident tribe is the persistent colonial stereotype. A. Skaria, *Hybrid Histories: Frontiers and Wildness in Western India*, Oxford University Press, (Delhi, 1999), p. 63; T. Sarkar, 'Jitu Santal's Movement in Malda in 1924-1932: A Study in Tribal Protest', *Subaltern Studies IV*, Oxford University Press, (Delhi, 1990), p. 147. The easy availability of land argued by the above British-day sources should not be fully accepted. The British forest policy of protection and reservation shrinked the area of Ho expansion. Moreover, the land alienation due to mining gradually intensified the problem. I have broached this in 'Singhbhum 1927-30'. About allergy to industrial work see LRAR for 1928-29, FL, DC's Office, GD, RD, CN XI, FN 19 of 1929, section 49.
53. C.B. Prasad, *Final Report on Survey and Settlement Operations in the District of Singhbhum, 1958-1965*, Secretariat Press, (Patna, 1970), pp. 63–70.
54. Roy Choudhury, *Bihar District Gazetteers*, pp. 245–59.
55. A recent study has challenged the 'romantic' idea of a 'Timeless Primitive'or changelessness in tribal society in the anthropological studies. Ronato Rosaldo, *Ilongot Headhunting 1883-1974: A Study in Society and History*, Stanford University Press, Stanford, (California, 1980), pp. 24–5.
56. A. Beteille, *Society and Politics in India – Essays in Comparative Perspective*, Oxford University Press, (Delhi, 1992), pp. 59–60.
57. S.C. Dube (ed) *Tribal Heritage of India*, Vol. I, Vikas Publishing House Pvt. Ltd., (New Delhi, 1977), p. 2.
58. K.S. Singh, *Tribal Society in India*, Manohar, (Delhi, 1985), p. 14.
59. D.N. Mazumdar, *Affairs of a Tribe*, (Calcutta, 1950), pp. 136, 48.

8

From Singhbhum to Assam: The Incidence of Labour Emigration 1873-1918

Migration constituted an almost recurrent and uninterrupted reality of tribal life in India.[1] However, what changed over time was its form and nature. It began with their withdrawal into the fastness of the hills and jungles after Aryan expansion into the more fertile territory tribals earlier inhabited.[2] This happened with the Kolarian people of Jharkhand who were forced to migrate from the Gangetic plain to the Chotanagpur plateau. At the next phase they dispersed into neighbouring districts of Bihar and Bengal when their Munda, Santal and Ho identities evolved over tracts they colonized by clearing adjacent forested spaces. But during the nineteenth century the subjugation of plateau region under British rule and the implementation of the colonial policy of reservation and protection of the woodland adversely affecting forest-cultivation dependent tribal socio-economy marginalized families had to stage inter-villlage and inter-*pir* migrations for a living. To this was added more distant movements to Calcutta and eastern parts of the country as plantation and factory labour as well as beyond the country.

The entire historical phenomenon of tribal migration is yet to be studied. Hopefully the rich body of archival materials has enabled initial researches into the migration of 'coolies and colliers' from Central India and Chotanagpur to tea gardens of Assam and the coalfields of Bihar and Bengal.[3] With varying focus these throw up important data about causes of emigration, its network, plantation-government nexus as promoting labour movement etc. With the tribal regions of Central Province and Chotanagpur in focus these works generally suffer from some obvious limitations. To substantiate, the focus on Chotanagpur is dispersed in the work of Bates and Carter, which concentrates on Central Provinces. Besides regional discrepancy, we notice inter-district discrepancy in Mohapatra[4] and Ghosh who neglect Singhbhum and the Ho when they take up Chotanagpur. This may be attributed to the author's (Mohapatra) dependence mainly on Craven and Tuckey Settlement Reports and other generic reports where facts about labour emigration to Assam from Singhbhum are meagre.[5] Moreover we notice the tendency of spatializing Chotanagpur-Santal Parganas as a unified tribal zone and that too as if having a singular past[6] when experiences were often spatio-demographically specific. To clarify my point, I would like to emphasize that varying incidence of land alienation and money lending as causing emigration elsewhere in Chotanagpur and Santal Parganas was not very relevant for the tribal parts of Singhbhum.

Keeping the particularity of Singhbhum in mind and with privileged access to the Village Papers this chapter presents an overview of labour emigration from this district to Assam elaborating the system of recruitment, quantum and cause of emigration, evils of the system and its impact on indigenous society. The author initiates this study from 1873, the year of the passing of the Labour Emigration Act. The account closes with the end of the Tuckey Settlement, which was a crucial event in the history of erstwhile Kolhan.

EMIGRATION: THE STRUCTURE

Emigration structure developed around Labour Emigration Act VII (BC) of 1873, Inland Emigration Act 1 of 1882, Act I (BC) of 1889 and Act VI of 1901[7], which replaced the preceding two Acts. During the period under review two modes of recruitment functioned. The first was regulated by the above Acts, while the other i.e. the free labour system did not function in accordance with the letter and spirit of the Act.[8] Labour was indentured both by contractors and certified garden *sardars* in Chotanagpur and Santal Parganas.[9] Similarly, while contractors and their recruiters recruited labour under Act VI of 1901 from Dhalbhum *pargana* of Singhbhum, certified garden *sardars* were allowed to recruit from Kolhan. This was extended to Porahat *pargana* also by the Notification No. 4768 of 5 November 1908.[10] Being the headquarters of Singhbhum district, Chaibasa was the official recruiting centre. In 1892, six '*coolie*' depots functioned in the town with the capacity to accommodate 329 recruits. This was raised to 350 the next year.[11] S.C. Ganguly, Barry & Company, Tapsy Singh, H.L. Mukherjee, Ghosal, Sen & Company and Mathu Sau were the recruiters of labour.[12] According to the Act of 1882 district magistrates were empowered to act as registering officers. But in some of the districts of Chotanagpur medical officers, stationed at the headquarters, were the registering officers.[13] In Singhbhum the Civil Surgeon, who was also the Assistant Commissioner, acted in that capacity.[14]

The free emigration system was a clandestine and extra legal system, which effectively competed with the official system. The ground reality was that the juridical divide of legal and free emigration was not often observed. Licensed contractors also acted as free recruiting agents and local agents for garden *sardars*.[15] The result was that free emigrants were often more in number than those recruited through the legal process. So the strong current of clandestine emigration did not always reflect the actual labour drain. The free labours were sent either direct to certain tea gardens for which they were specially decoyed, or they were routed through their agents in Raniganj and Calcutta. In Singhbhum *deshi sardars* and contractors of Midnapur generally did the illicit recruitment.[16] Moreover, the organisations like the Tea Districts Labour Supply Association[17] recruited Singhbhum labour through its depot at Chaibasa, which was practically a rest house for its free *sardars* and their labourers before being registered at Purulia.[18] Legal process of obtaining recruiting licenses was evaded obviously for the expense and hazard involved in routing labour through Chaibasa.[19] Labourers moved through two different rail-routes. One was to reach Dhubri via Asansol, Hooghly, Naihati, Sharaghat and Kaunia. The other was to travel via Calcutta to Goalundo and from there to Dhubri. Those to Surma Valley i.e. Cachar and Sylhet reached Goalundo by the second route from where they boarded the steamer to reach their destinations.[20]

The Acts of 1882 and 1889 and a set of 26 rules framed in 1889-90 regulated the inland emigration system. Emigrating agencies were supposed to provide sufficient food, drinking water and accommodation to labourers at the depot and during journey, to make proper sanitary and medical arrangements, to treat them if they fell sick on their way and also to make other arrangements to render their journey comfortable. Periodic inspection of rest houses and depots by responsible officers was enjoined. In case of violation of the rules provision for imposing a fine up to Rs. 500 was made.[21] But the colonial government seemed more eager to protect the tea industry in Assam from the spread of plague, cholera, small pox and other contagious diseases through these recruits rather than providing necessary facilities. This concern was articulated and arrangements for the segregation of '*coolies*' affected by such diseases on their way to Assam were made at Sara, Naihati and various halting stations.[22]

THE NUMBER—CONFUSION AND CONFLATION

During early years the number of emigrants from Singhbhum was not considerable. This was because people in general were not normally favourable to emigration, as majority of them was believed to be well off.[23] It seems that emigration began in the 1870s as the figures of 444 labourers in 1877 and 410 in 1878 show.[24] Table 8.1 reveals first a marked rise later, though it was much lower than the divisional figure.[25] Secondly, the number generally dwindled between 1879-85 with fluctuations during next five years. This may largely be attributed to the failure in appropriating the exact figure of emigrants through free system. Years of which figures of free labourers available clearly show that the non-official system often swamped the government managed, which perhaps explains the official number dwindling to 1 during 1886.

Table 8.1

Year	*Registered*	*Free*	*Year*	*Registered*	*Free*
1879-80	038		1885-86	41	
1880-81	609		1886-87	1	
1881-82	896		1887-88	68	
1882-83	386		1888-89	33	254
1883-84	227	548	1889-90	98	385
1884-85	38				

Source: AGARCD, 1881-2, No. 14T, 30 June 1882, para 33, CN XIV Misc. FN 1 AGARCD, p. 10, Government of Bengal, GD Misc. November 1887, FN 155, pp. 520-82; AGARCD, p. 9, Proceedings of the Government of Bengal, GD, Misc. October 1890, FN 149, pp. 65–108.

Another trend was the fluctuation in number and the rise in the quinquennium average of the number of emigrants. This can be understood from the Table 8.2.[26]

Table 8.2

Years	Number	Year	Number
1901-2	978	1906-07	593
1902-3	1457	1907-08	3033
1903-4	824	1908-09	4454
1904-5	634	1909-10	2055
1905-6	866	1910-11	1875

The quinquennium average for 1901 to 1905-6 rose from 951.8 to 2402 for 1906-7 to 1910-11. The fluctuation was assigned to failure of crops and consequent rise in price and the subsequent return of normalcy and prosperity.[27] But it appears that rise might also be due to the practice of labourers of neighbouring feudatory states of Mayurbhanj, Gangpur, Bonai, Keonjhar, Seraikela, Kharsawan and other unnamed districts being routed through Chaibasa. Out of the total of 3033 and 4454 recruits in 1907-8 and 1908-9, 1117 and 905 respectively belonged to the princely states.[28] This trend continued later. Nearly half the total of 1875 in 1910-11, 500 out of 1606 in 1913-4, larger number of 1537 in 1914-5, 5098 out of 15477 in 1916-7, 2831 of 4890 in 1917-8 were from the neighbouring feudatory states and districts.[29] This usurpation definitely gave a misleading figure for Singhbhum. Moreover, it clearly proved that the local administration was deliberately encouraging recruitment from the princely states against the wishes of the chiefs and avowed official policy enunciated in the Notification of 1879 of discouraging clandestine recruitment.[30]

This encouragement perhaps operated within the official illusion that emigration was a moral act[31], which besides promoting the industry itself laterally obviated distress through employment. During 1907-9, the administration promoted *sardari* recruitment by granting concession to *sardars* working under various recognized associations[32], raising the figure to the high of 4454 in 1908-9 from 593 in 1906-7. Failure to provide separate figures for registered and free '*coolies*' is another noticeable feature presented by Table 8.2. Singhbhum '*coolies*', being sent to Ranigunj and Calcutta under free system instead of their being registered at Chaibasa[33], inflated the figures of Manbhum and Midanpur and deflated that of Singhbhum.

It was officially claimed that internal demand of labour created by the Tata Company at Sakchi, iron mines in Dhalbhum and Kolhan, copper mines at Matigara, railway works, lac factories at Chaibasa and Chakradharpur reduced the over-dependence of people on agriculture and caused decline in emigration.[34] The aggregate of 34980 computed from the following table as contrasted from that of 12876 during 1905-11 (Table 8.2) however challenges the above claim.

Table 8.3

Years	*Emigrants*
1912-3	2136
1913-4	1606
1914-5	1537
1915-6	9334
1916-7	15477
1917-8	4890

Source: LRAR for 1913-14, entry No. XLIX; LRAR for 1914-15, entry No. LXIX. However there is some confusion, LRAR 1914-15 shows 1329 as the figure for the last year i.e. 1913-4, while 1606 is the number shown in LRAR for the year 1913-4. Similarly, 11458 is the figure for the last year (1916-17) in LRAR 1917-8, when LRAR for 1916-7 shows that the figure for the year is 15477.

Another uncertainty is in respect of age or sex distribution. Figures given in Table 8.4 only divide the number between labourers and their dependants who accompanied them, neither their sex nor age.

Table 8.4

Years	*Labourers*	*Dependants*
1902-3	923	534
1903-4	546	278
1905-6	543	323

Source: LRAR 1903-4, DC's Office, GD, RB, CN XIII Annual Returns, FN 8, p. 48; LRAR 1904-5, DC's Office, GD, RB, CN XIII AR & Reports, FN 6, entry 48/48A; LRAR, 1906-7, DC's Office, GD, RB, CN XI

Returns, FN 12, entry 48.

It means that out of a total of 3147 emigrants for these years 2012 were actual labourers i.e. 64 per cent of the total volume of emigration, while the rest were their dependants. Bereft of data about the sex and age, though, what we gather relates that the nature of emigration from Singhbhum was family migration like other districts of Chotanagpur.[35] So this 'family colonization', as seen elsewhere[36], helped create a homely atmosphere at their work places which prevented possible desertion due to 'home sickness'.

The colonial government considered the Labour of Chotanagpur and Santal Parganas most suited for tea gardens of Assam.[37] They were preferred to those from the North Western Provinces mainly because of their relative docility. This was reflected in the higher wage-rate of Rs. 120 in 1895 for pure aboriginal labourers compared to Rs. 60 paid to NWP '*coolies*'.[38] The Mundas, Oraons, Kharias, Hos, Bhumijs, Santals, Kurmis, Murasis, Ghasis, Goraits, Bauris, Turis, Bhogtas, Rautias, Chamars and Dosadhs constituted the bulk of the recruits. The Mundas were the largest among them, followed by the Oraons and Ghasis.[39] We do not, however, have detailed information about the ethnic or social roots of Singhbhum emigrants. Even then a tentative attempt may be made to explore their identities.

With varying emphasis the migration to Assam is believed to have been caused by economic distress caused by land alienation, indigence of small cultivators, occurrence of famines, the absence of work during lean seasons[40] as well as such cultural factors[41] as the pressure of the cost of marriage and marginalization of women in a patriarchal setting. The next is the role of colonial government often acting in tandem to promote capitalism by ensuring the smooth and steady supply of labour as per its requirements.[42] On the other hand, Mohapatra enumerated such causes of labour emigrations as demand of plantation labour, the economic condition in the labour catchment areas, lack of expansion of cultivation, rent burden, indebtedness and the impact of ecology.[43]

What do we find if we test the above factors in the context of Singhbhum? Mohapatra, who appears to be more relevant for the obvious reason, did not find demand factor to be relevant for entire Chotanagpur. This essay is unable to study the correlation due to the paucity of information. About the second factor, like other districts Singhbhum also registered a steady growth in cultivation, which was to the extent of 80 per cent between 1867 and 1897 and 29 per cent between 1897 and 1918.[44] So lack of expansion of cultivation was not a valid reason. Debt burden was not officially considered a factor. Craven wrote about the Ho 'He lives cheaply and his wants are few. He is very seldom in debt.'[45] The official, however, seemed to underestimate the problem of indebtedness in Kolhan. The correlation between indebtedness and emigration cannot be completely ruled out because of the fact that in Kolhan villages many of the mortgagors ended up migrating to Assam.[46] The impact of bad harvests had been underlined as the major rather the only cause in the generic colonial records on Singhbhum.[47] While the specific ones on the villages similarly held famine conditions responsible for emigration from Kolhan villages, e.g. Khandkhori, Usambir and Patahatu.[48] But the reality was that scarcity or famine did not cause emigration as instanced by the neighbouring Haldia village.[49] Moreover, even in the above three villages the rate of migrants in respect of total population, except for Khandkhori, was inconsiderable.[50] So a reason more decisive has to be explored.

In this context Mohapatra's ecological factor merits an examination. He suggests in the case of Chotanagpur that the areas, where *don* III land constituted a large proportion of the net cultivated area, were the worst affected. People of the region could not sustain the crisis of bad harvests and were forced to emigrate to Assam.[51] In a recent study it has been shown that geomorphology immensely influences the density of agriculture and the crop pattern in Singhbhum. Singhbhum, both east and west, as well as Mayurbhanj and Keonjhar districts of Orissa form part of the Kharkai basin. This basin is divided into different geomorphic units i.e. scarp zones, plantation surfaces, accidental relief areas and valleys. In the scarp zones the percentage of land under cultivation is insignificant. Moreover, highlands and scarp zones grow crops, which require less moisture, as maize etc. On the other hand, the plains of the district mainly grow rice.[52] This hypothesis cannot, however, be historically related to show the pattern and growth in cultivation for lack of further knowledge. We only know that in Singhbhum *gora* or third class land constituted 42 per cent of the total cultivated area.[53] As the village-wise information about emigration is not available the susceptibility of families inhabiting low cultivation areas or owning the third class of land in greater proportion to the owners of the first two classes cannot be definitely established.

We have yet another factor, which should be examined to explain

Singhbhum-situation. This factor is the marginality of smaller peasantry. Obviously failing to sustain the adverse effects of crop failure Singhbhum *raiyats* with small holdings[54], both from tribal and non-tribal families, had to mortgage their frail holdings and leave for Assam. The Diku Reports of different Mankis' *elakas* instanced such migrations by the Tantis, Hos and some Goalas.[55] Emigration idea had penetrated even Kolhan, rather insulated part of the district. The Village Notes relating to the Tuckey Settlement record 282 recruitments from 36 villages with the highest of 74 from Khandkhori village of Lalgarh *pir* alone.[56] The case of Khandkhori may be taken up to elaborate my point further.

The soil of this village belonged to three classes, *Gitil* i.e. sandy soil, *Arahasa* i.e. sandy soil containing sand in a smaller quantity and *Rugudhasa* i.e. rocky soil. There was little artificial irrigation in the village where only 40 *bighas* of paddy fields were irrigated. Paddy lands were generally manured annually but not *gora* lands. The village was inhabited by 716 people, out of whom 492 were the Hos and 224 were Tantis, Kamars, Goalas and Doms. Out of a total area of 2150-18-15 *bighas*, rice land constituted 1045-18-6, upland i.e. *gora* or *tanr* 1031-9-15 and uncultivated land 73-10-14 *bighas*.[57] The distribution of land holdings is shown in Table 8.5.

Table 8.5

Land (in bigha)	Ho	Non-Ho	Land (in bigha)	Ho	Non-Ho
Less than 1	11	7	40-50	9	
Less than 10	56	11	50-60	1	
10-20	30	1	60-70	1	
20-30	22		80-90	1	
30-40	8				

Source: Tuckey Settlement, Class A, File A, In the Court of the Revenue Officer of Kolhan, Suit or Case No. 88/85 (2) ii of 1917, *Secretary of State for India-in-Council* Vs. *Raiyats* of Village Khandkhori, pp. 5–23.

It shows that 85 holdings were below 10 *bighas*. Out of them those having holdings with greater quantity of upland and uncultivated land were more prone to emigration. Even in higher brackets those with lesser quantum of rice land were no less emigration-prone. So this village may somewhat explicate the social root of the emigrants. In this context the marginality of the non-Hos becomes very evident.

We learn that the *dikus* of this village owned in all a paltry 63-12-16 *bighas* of land, none of whom possessed more than 20 *bighas*. About their material condition it was remarked 'The areas at present held by the foreigners is not at all sufficient for their maintenance. Most of them maintain themselves by labour.'[58]

Though not directly involved the colonial forest policy should be held partially responsible in two ways. First, that large forest areas being progressively demarcated as reserved and protected the earlier Ho expansion into the forests for creating new cultivating spaces to obviate the pressure of growing population on village lands was stopped. As a result, the pressure on the existing land increased considerably. Secondly, during crop failure Ho society was deprived of the indigenous mechanism of distress relief through the use of forest produce. These aggravated the situation forcing social marginals to migrate.[59]

Generally, recruiters were local people who worked as garden *sardars* or *arkatis*. We come across one instance of itinerant recruiters from Assam visiting Kolhan.[60] The period of recruitment in Singhbhum was generally for either four or five years.[61] But the period of contract did not always reflect the period of absence of the migrant labourer from his village. Matkam Ho of Sarkand village went to Assam shortly after Craven Settlement[62], Ganeswar Tanti of Khariatanger left 8 years ago[63] and Kudu Tanti of Bharbharia 12 years before.[64] Absence of information of their subsequent return proves that their migrant state lasted longer than the stipulated period of engagement. But it is difficult to make out whether it was fraudulent detention by the employer or economic distress at home that caused this overstay.[65]

FAULTS AND THEIR CORRECTIONS

The government intended the recruiting system to function like a well-oiled machine to ensure steady and uninterrupted supply of labour. But in spite of rules and superintendence the system was honeycombed with abuses. The forcible kidnapping or abduction, enticement of both males and females by fraud or misrepresentation were reported from Chotanagpur.[66] The planters seemed particularly interested in young women obviously not simply for tea gardens. It is reported: 'Considerable pressure is put upon local agents and their subordinates to procure a supply of women for the tea gardens and this of course gives rise to great abuses.'[67] Mode of enticement at the local level becomes clear from the following cases. Potu Gourin and Mango Uraoin were brought to Chakradharpur by garden *sardars* named Mirdha and Birsa Ho, with the promise of keeping them as their mistresses but in reality to despatch them as '*coolies*' to Assam. The fraudulent emigration of one Jingi Kolin, a woman of 20 years, by Sadhu Kol and Arjun Gour with the similar promise was attempted. More such cases are also reported.[68]

Proper sanitary and medical arrangements proved to be the other achilles heel. Labourers suffering from fever, diarrhea, dysentery and cholera was a regular phenomenon often causing death to many.[69] Sanitary and health facilities at European managed depots were reported to be satisfactory as compared to sub-standard state at labour depots under Indian management.[70] But claim of superiority of the European management was preposterous in view of the fact that there was indeed no management exclusively Indian or European as such as shown by Chaibasa depots. These depots were reported to be under the regular vigil of the Civil Surgeon and District Superintendent of Police and periodically of the Deputy Commissioner himself. Yet there was no special water supply or sanitary arrangement. Inmates had to depend on the river nearby for water.[71]

As the government believed that the official system was free from evil local administration merely attempted reform of the free emigration system. The illicit recruitment was countered by the cancellation of the contract of the defaulter.[72] The authorization and identification of all *arkatis*, recruiters and sub-agents by their employers and the licensing and registering of them by the magistrate of the district in which they had been authorized to recruit were suggested.[73] To make superintendence and control more full proof the government appointed Travelling Superintendent of Emigration for Bengal and Central Provinces with headquarters at Purulia. Moreover, 5 Superintendents were appointed one each for Ranchi and Palamau, Singhbhum and Manbhum, Hazaribagh, Santal Parganas and the remaining districts of Bengal.[74] Medical inspection of emigrants at Mugra, Jaipurhat, Dhubri, Goalundo and Narayanganj was arranged.[75]

Regular doses of reform however failed to set things right. This shook the confidence of the Government of India, which failing to enforce the Superintendent of Emigration's proposal of compulsory local registration of recruits, was compelled to prescribe the natural cure of the wrong. To quote 'If the evil of misdescription increases to any great extent, it will develop its own remedy.'[76] This also failed to deliver the goods. Dismayed Governor-General-in-Council detected that the local administration was in fact responsible for the failure. It was communicated: 'In this, as in other matters relating to the working of the Emigration System, the benevolent intention of the legislature are of little avail if they are not seconded and intelligently enforced by the district executive.'[77]

SOCIAL IMPACT

Five years' agreement on a pay of Rs. 5 or 6, and Rs. 7 if under free agents[78], no doubt provided some relief to the already beleaguered marginalized families. When rice sold at 14 *seers* and 8 *chatak* per rupee in the years 1903-5[79], for example, this pay was not inconsiderable.[80] So the lure of a job even in strange and distant Assam was so irresistible for some people of Kolhan that men or women, Ho or *diku*, came to accept it as a lucrative alternative vocation. But not improvidence alone, even those like Dinoo Ho of Gumria who had more than 19 *bighas* of land, perhaps not insignificant in Kolhan, or Suna Ho who had social status and additional source of income as the Munda of Gotsereng[81], also preferred to emigrate. But why did they do so remained unanswered in the village records.

The job prospect was carroted before the needy and willing at their immediate or not too distant neighbourhood. In Darposhi village of Bar *pir* one Myres opened a labour depot with the permission of the Munda in the 1890s.[82] Marki Munda of Diliamarcha settled a *gora* land with Walker for a labour depot.[83] Moreover, Chaibasa depots were always the haven for those interested. Through these exotic institutions both official and free trade expanded. *Arkatis*, both *diku* and Ho men and women, were always there to throw the noose on the willing or unwilling. Magan Tamaria of Suiamba went to Assam in 1903, he returned to his village two years later as a garden *sardar* to recruit.[84] Magan was perhaps in legitimate labour trade but not Sheikh Idu from Gaya and his two Dom women accomplices. They enticed away a woman of Jagannathpur. Complaint was lodged that several men and women had been decoyed by untrained *sardars*.[85] Under the cover of other legitimate business some were also engaged in illegal labour traffic. Sohrai Tamaria of Kokcho, for example, acted as an *arkati* though he was ostensibly a lac trader.[86] Jano Kolin complained to the district administration that Bangra and Gurucharan Kamar and Dula and Gardi Ho had secretly *challaned* her son Borju and her husband's brother Pasing Ho to Assam.[87] So some people of Kolhan came to accept the job of a labour or decoy as employment opportunity.[88] Though marginally, labour traffic to Assam added a new item in the existing employment corpus of tilling, labour in land, mines and the railways as well as various caste professions.

Emigration however caused social distress. Ghasiram Ho of Udajo left for Assam in 1880, he returned only during the Craven Settlement.[89] But some like Pandu Ho of Kharband was not recorded as having ever returned.[90] When a father or husband emigrated the family life was disturbed. This happened when Duroo Ho of Ulidih left his wife and son behind or Fakir Gour his son.[91] It saddled the lady with the responsibility to earn the bread. This also brought in its trail other problems. Randoi Kui was married to a recorded *raiyat* of Bhetia. When her husband went away to Assam she returned to her paternal village with her sons. Her material position changed as her husband's land came in the physical possession of her husband's brother and from a land owning *raiyat*'s wife she became a labourer.[92] Suru Kui's case provides another but different kind of status change. After her husband left for Assam, Suru had to move to her brother's house at Burijol with her children. While she was a recorded *raiyat* of Horlor, her husband's village, she was declared to be a *diku* for Burijol.[93]

Land alienation through mortgage, sale or temporary surrender of possession to a relation or others was natural and endemic.[94] Consequent court cases for recovery of land became an order of the day. But as against such willful transfers by the owner, forcible change of title was not infrequent. Dunoo Ho of Dumria had mortgaged his 7 *bigha* 7 *katha* and 5 *dhur* land to Jiba Ho on a payment of Rs. 4. But as he did not return from Assam after eight years his land was mutated in Jiba's name.[95] Similarly on Mungroo Ho leaving for Assam shortly after Craven Settlement his lands were settled with others.[96] The government was found too eager to obviate revenue loss. So when a land remained uncultivated or rent unpaid or title was unclaimed or uncertain, mutation applied for generally met with favour. Moreover, the twelve-year criterion was introduced during Craven Settlement for entitlement. Ten plots of land belonging to Damo Ho thus passed to Bara Jiba Ho as his father Raro was in continuous possession of them for twelve years on Damo leaving for Assam.[97] But not land alone, Lakhindar Ho, the eldest son of Hurdub Munda of Pardi, lost the Mundaship for which he was the legal heir as he was away to Assam when his father died. As his other brother declined the offer the post moved to Hurdub's brother's family.[98]

Assam emigration also affected the mentality of the Hos of Kolhan. Due to indigence the inter-village or inter-*pir* or migration to neighbouring Keonjhar and Mayurbhanj districts was a social phenomenon. But prospect of job and better life made far off Assam tea gardens the *el dorado* for some. This marked the beginning of the culture of labour migration to distant Assam or other provinces of India. This was a clear departure from what Dalton wrote in 1872: 'The Larkas are lightly assessed, and cultivating their own lands, never join any of the numerous band of labourers emigrating to tea districts. They refuse to hear the voice of the recruiter, claim he never so enticingly'.[99]

Labour trade involved great amount of deceit and fraud. In this a Ho or a *diku* unscrupulously combined in camaraderie in crime. This inoculated an otherwise simple and innocent Ho with the doses of deceit, fraud and a brazen cut throat attitude. As a result community affiliation, softness towards females which Hayes or Dalton found[100] or Tickell-day non-material and carefree worldview[101] surrendered before material gain. They were gradually conditioned to a new notion of criminality. Commitment of murder or suicide due to sudden on-rush of blood[102] was joined by cool and calculated act of deception and seduction.

This also intensified the aura of suspicion and mistrust in an otherwise open and transparent world of Kolhan, particularly of the tribals. Society expected everything to be visible and above board. A source of living had to be ostensible; a man must be found to work for a living and the life style proportionate to the profession pursued. Any departure from this norm created doubt in a man, causing villagers to suspect him to be either a thief or anti-social. The past record of an abnormal act finally fixated the irreputable image on the person. Other than the occult world of witches and sorcerers, labour trade therefore further infected Kolhan openness with creeping suspicion about the genuineness of a being and his vocation. One case would illustrate my point. Jano Kolin complained against two Kamars and Hos each of deceitfully deputing Barju and Pasing Ho to Assam pretending to send them to Chakradharpur as porters.

Though the charge could not be proved after official investigation, the accused persons were kept under surveillance. But how the atmosphere of suspicion was woven and criminal personification of the suspected was made appear interesting. One of the accused Dula Ho owned lands in the village. But he had borrowed Rs. 300 from a man of Chaibasa, which he failed to repay. Moreover, he had taken settlement of a *pachai* shop but could not do so the next year. These showed that he was avaricious and was trying to live beyond his ostensible source of earning through cultivation, both socially deplorable. So when villagers found that he was in friendship with 'coolie' recruiters they suspected him to be an active decoy. Dula's cousin Gadai Ho was more prone to social suspicion. He had no land of his own, so no known source of earning. This was accentuated by his murky past. Gadai and Jota Ho of San Guira had attempted to deport one Kolin of Harila to Assam. Jota was prosecuted while Gadai escaped to Porahat. Two other suspects were Bengra and Gurucharan Kamars, co-villagers of the above. While the former had merely less than one *bigha* land, the latter had none. Bengra did not cultivate, nor was he seen to work, nor did he live in the village. Everything about his existence was therefore clandestine, opaque and so suspicious. Yet he was an itinerant man. All these prompted people to suspect that he visited villages only to recruit 'coolies'. Villagers also came to believe that he had gone to Assam once. But more compelling reason was that both the brothers had before been convicted for sending a woman of Saidba to Assam. For this particular reason the villagers linked them to the illegal migration of Matoo Ho of Nimdih to Assam or all combined inspired Jano Kolin's complaint to the local administration.[103]

This suspicion shows a social bias against those engaged in labour traffic even though migration had been taking place. In fact, the normal trend was that people disliked this act. The Diku Reports recorded that villagers who acted either as *arkatis* or *sardars* were socially despised and the grudge was articulated before inspecting officials.[104] This made a tribal or *diku* an undesirable element in the village community paving the way for his possible ouster from the village. This also shows that emigration was socially considered a detestable act challenging the colonial government's attempt to project it as a benevolent and socially accepted measure to ameliorate social distress through employment. The ambivalence in Kolhan society was replicated by British government's oscillation between softness to emigration trade to promote tea industry and avowed protection of Kolhan Hos in their hearth and home. So, on the one hand, the government encouraged labour emigration by allowing labour depots to run in the interior of Kolhan and at Chaibasa. But on the other, it initiated the process of branding unlicensed hide trade and labour emigration as an illegitimate trade under the Thomson's Rules of 1903[105] and passing orders for expulsion against many for their association in labour traffic to Assam.[106]

NOTES

1. This is the dominant theme of tribal oral tradition as narrated by Guru Kolean, see P.O. Bodding (Tr.), *Traditions and Institutions of the Santals/ Horkoren Mare Hapramko Raek Katha,* Bahumukhi Prakashan, Indian Reprint, (New Delhi, 1994).
2. D.D. Kosambi, *An Introduction to the Study of Indian History*, Popular Prakashan, Bombay, 1985, pp. 110–14.
3. I would like to particularly name C. Bates and M. Carter, 'Tribal Migration in India and Beyond' in Gyan Prakash (ed.), *The World of the Rural Labourer in Colonial India*, OUP, (Delhi, 1994) (1992); 'Tribal and Indentured Migrants in Colonial India: Modes of Recruitment and Forms of Incorporation', in P. Robb, (ed.). *Dalit Movements and the Meanings of Labour in India,* OUP, (Delhi, 1999) (1993); K. Ghosh, 'A Market for Aboriginality: Primitivism and Race Classification in the Indentured Labour Market of Colonial India' in G. Bhadra, Gyan Prakash and S. Tharu, (eds.), *Subaltern Studies X*, OUP, (Delhi, 2000), (1999); Mohapatra, 'Coolies and Colliers'.
4. P.P. Mohapatra's revealing study on labour emigration from Chotanagpur to Assam shows that from Hazaribagh, Ranchi, Palamau, Manbhum and Singhbhum districts of this division the number of migrants rose from 1,90,012 in 1891 to 3,00,561 in 1921 census. Of these districts the larger share belonged to Ranchi, Manbhum and Hazaribagh followed by Singhbhum and Palamau. Mohapatra, 'Coolies and Colliers', pp. 250–51. In this wider spectrum of study, which also includes migrants to coal mines of Jharia in Manbhum, Singhbhum makes a cursory presence.
5. Ibid., pp. 251–2.
6. I have in mind the overblown Dhangar metaphor in Ghosh, 'A Market for Aboriginality', pp. 17–8.
7. Prior to 1873, Act of 1863 and Act VI of 1865 were passed by the Bengal Council that laid the emigration structure. R.P. Behal and P.P. Mohapatra, 'Tea and Money versus Human Life: The Rise and Fall of the Indenture System in the Assam Tea Plantation 1840-1908', *The Journal of Peasant Studies*, Vol. 19, No. 1, October 1991, p. 146.

8. Memorandum regarding recruiting submitted by J. Buckingham, Chairman, Assam Branch, India Tea Association, p. 1, vide C.E. Buckland, Secretary to the Government of Bengal, to the Commissioner of Chotanagpur Division, GD, Inland Emigration No. 90 TG, 7 June 1892, FL, CN II Emigration, FN 2 of 1892.
9. S.R. Hignell (Compiler), *The Administration of the Lower Provinces of Bengal during the Lieutenant Governorship of Sir John Woodburn, being a supplement to Annual General Administration Report for 1901-02*, Bengal Secretariat Press, (Calcutta, 1903), p. 44. Recruitment structure changed over the years. Since the 1860s, labour was recruited by licensed European contractors through their Indian agents and garden *sardars* with the provision of registration of the recruits in their related districts. Act 1882 introduced the system of free and deregulated emigration. As a result old agencies of licensed contractors and recruiters suffered. The new system was headed by the Calcutta Managing houses which functioned with the help of local agents. These in turn had their sadar *arkattis* under them, the latter operating through the *arkattis* or village recruiters. Behal and Mohapatra, 'Tea and Money', pp. 150–2.
10. Quinquennial Administration Report of the Chotanagpur Division for the period ending the 31 March 1910, Nos. 11-12, File 5-R/6, para 21, Proceedings of the Government of Bengal, GD, Miscellaneous, April 1911.
11. Deputy Commissioner, Singhbhum to Commissioner, Chhotanagpur Division, 4 March 1893, para 2, Annual Return of Accommodation of Coolies, FL, CN I Emigration, FN 3.
12. Deputy Commissioner, Singhbhum's Note of 8 September 1900 and Head Clerk N.C. Tripathy's reply of 10 September 1900 on Report on the result of inspection of the accommodations for free emigrants, FL, CN IV AR, FN 18 of 1900.
13. T.W. Richardson, Officiating Under Secretary to the Government of Bengal, to the Commissioner of Chotanagpur, para 2, GD Emigration, 12 August, 1892, CN II Emigration, FN 4 of 1892.
14. Head Clerk N.C. Tripathy's note to Dy. Commissioner, Singhbhum, 14 May 1891, vide Commissioner, Chotanagpur's Memo No. 1 of 21 May 1891, para 8, FL, CN II Emigration, FN 1 of 1891.
15. Memorandum regarding recruiting, p. 1.
16. GAR for 1883-84, Singhbhum district, para 18; Note on the history of Singhbhum district during the decade 1901-11, p. 25 (page numbering by author), FL, CN, VII, FN 25 of 1911-12.
17. It was a centralised recruiting agency which since 1902 did the major recruiting work through the garden *sardars*. Behal and Mohapatra, 'Tea and Money', p. 167.
18. Allan Mathewson to C.H. Bompas, Officiating Dy. Commissioner, Singhbhum, 7 April 1896, para 1, 22 April 1896, para 1, GD, Emigration Branch No. 182 JH, Construction of Coolie depots, FL, CN IX Emigration,

FN 2. Purulia was the major recruiting centre in Chotanagpur. Behal and Mohapatra, 'Tea and Money', p. 152.

19. Note on the history, p. 24.
20. Dy. Commissioner, Singhbhum's draft of a letter to Commissioner, Chotanagpur Division, 1 January1892, FL, CN II Emigration, FN 1 of 1891.
21. Rules issued in addition to the existing rules under Act 1 (BC) of 1889, Notification 28 May 1889 and 23 December 1890 vide Commissioner, Chotanagpur's office Memo No. J-121, 4 May 1891, FL, CN II Emigration, FN 1, 1891, GD Inland Emigration Resolution No. 63 of 25 April 1891, para 1, Ibid.
22. GD Emigration, Resolution No. 2135, 20 July 1899 para 2, Report on Emigration, FL, CN IV Annual Returns, FN 9 of 1899.
23. GAR of 1883-84, para 17.On the whole this seems to be a pan-Chotanagpur phenomenon. Ghosh, 'A Market for Aboriginality', p. 29.
24. GAR 1878-9, Singhbhum District, No. 678, Chaibasa, May 1879, p. 9.
25. Small compared to Chotanagpur in general from where 25614 migrated to Assam in 1878-9. Ghosh, 'A Market for Aboriginality', p. 30.
26. LRAR for 1908-9, entry No. 48B, GD, CN XI Return, FN 10 of 1908-9; LRAR, for 1916-17, entry No. XLIX, GD, CN XI Return, FN 1 of 1917.
27. Note on the history of Singhbhum, p. 28.
28. Quinquennial Administratin Report, para 22.
29. LRAR for 1910-11 entry No. XLIX, GD, CN XI, FN 1 of 1911-12; LRAR for 1913-4, entry No. XLIX, GD, CN XI, FN 1 of 1913-4; LRAR for 1914-5, entry No. XLIX, GD, CN XI Return, FN 8 of 1914-5; LRAR for 1916-7, entry No. XLIX, GD, CN XI Return, FN 1 of 1917; LRAR for1917-18, entry No. XLIX, GD, CN XI Return, FN 2 of 1918.
30. A.A. Wace, Officiating Commissioner, Chotanagpur Division to Dy. Commissioner, Singhbhum, No. 178, 15 October 1892, para 2, FL, CN II Emigration, FN 1 of 1892.
31. This idea prevailed both in respect of overseas and inland migration. It was believed that Mauritius outlet would provide job openings for 'hill coolies' wandering for jobs and for the Santhals migration was considered an escape from moneylenders. Bates, and Carter, 'Tribal and Indentured Migrants', p. 167. This was akin to planter's thinking: 'When the coolie goes to a garden he begins to live, whereas in Chotanagpur… he only exists.' Behal and Mohapatra, 'Tea and Money', p. 143.
32. Quinquennial Administration Report, para 22.
33. Note on the history of Singhbhum, pp. 24–5.
34. LRAR for 1909-10, entry No. XXI; Note on the history of Singhbhum, pp. 14, 16.
35. Mohapatra, 'Coolies and Colliers', p. 259.
36. Ghosh, 'A Market for Aboriginality', pp. 41–3.
37. The tea industry of Assam districts required labourers in great number for which Chotanagpur and Santal Parganas became fertile recruiting ground

touching roughly the height of 93 per cent of the total in 1901. Hignell, *The Administration of the Lower Provinces of Bengal*, pp. 44–6.

38. Mohapatra, 'Coolies and Colliers', pp. 264–5.
39. Ibid., p. 259.
40. Bates and Carter, 'Tribal Migration', pp. 218, 225.
41. Ibid., p. 224fn.
42. Bates and Carter, 'Tribal and Indentured Migrants', pp. 160–1.
43. Mohapatra, 'Coolies and Colliers', pp. 254–95.
44. Tuckey, *Final Report*, pp. 2, 4.
45. Craven, *Final Report*, p. 22.
46. This may be gleaned from Craven and Tuckey Settlement Village Papers containing *Thika* Lists.
47. LRAR 1903-4, pp. 87, 90.
48. TSVN, Vol. IV (301–400), pp. 133, 148, 154.
49. Ibid., p. 141.
50. In Khandhkori 74 out of 716 villagers, in Usambir 2 out of 124 and in Patahatu 14 out of 206 took the Assam-route. Ibid., pp. 133, 148, 154.
51. Mohapatra, 'Coolies and Colliers', p. 295.
52. D.N. Mahto, 'Geomorphology of the Kharkai Basin', (Ranchi University, Ph.D. Thesis, May 1998).
53. Craven, *Final Report*, p. 23.
54. Note on the history of Singhbhum, p. 17.
55. DR of the *elaka* of Gangaram Manki, FL, R/1071 of 1912-3, Misc. Case No. 718 of 1911-2, p. 3; DR of the *elaka* of Paikrai Manki, FL, R/995 of 1911-12, Misc. Case No. 543 of 1911-2, p. 5; DR of the *elaka* of Tusa Manki, FL. R/126 of 1911-2, Misc, Case No. 58 of 1910-11, pp. 13–5.
56. TSVN, Thana Nos. 301-400, pp. 11-685.
57. Ibid., pp. 129–30; TS, Class A File A, In the Court of the Revenue Officer of Kolhan, Suit or Case No. 88/85 (2) ii of 1917, *Secretary of State for India-in-Council* vs. *Raiyats of Village Khandhkori*, p. 23.
58. TSVN, *op. cit.*, pp. 134–5.
59. Though appearing strange famine affected those parts of Kolhan less severely which were agriculture-forest dependent compared to those more advanced agriculturally. 'Differential Peasantisation and the Changing Socio-Economy of the Ho Tribe of Singhbhum', section on Differential Peasantisation. Paper presented at the Seminar on the Changing Scenario of the Tribals and Indigenous People of Jharkhand, Bihar, West Bengal and Orissa, at *The Asiatic Society*, Kolkata on 8 January 2003.
60. DR of the *elaka* of Tusa Manki, FL. R/126 of 1911-2, Misc, Case No. 58 of 1910 –11, pp. 20-1; DR of the *elaka* of Gardi Manki, FL, R/625 of 1912-3, Misc. Case No. 545 of 1911-2, p. 4; DR of the *elaka* of Turam Manki, FL, R/1018 of 1912-3, Misc. Case No. 324 of 1912-3, p. 19; DR of the *elaka* of Borea Manki, FL, R/1024 of 1912-3, Misc. Case No. 456 of 1911-2, p. 39.
61. A statement showing the periods of service for which *sardari* emigrants

were placed on contract in the Singhbhum district for the Labour District during the calendar year of 1886, FL, CN III, FN 1, of 1887.

62. DR, R/1024, pp. 3–4.
63. Ibid., R/995, pp. 3–4.
64. Ibid., R/995, pp. 3–4.
65. One reason for overstay, perhaps causing permanent migration, was the practice of better term of employment enjoyed by the time-expired coolies. They received higher wage, a bonus, better service conditions and sometimes land for cultivation. Behal and Mohapatra, 'Tea and Money', pp. 147-48, 164.
66. C.E. Buckland, Secy. to the Government of Bengal, to the Secy. to the Govt. of India, Revenue and Agricultural Department, GD, Inland Emigration TC, June 1892, para 3, FL, CN II, Emigration, FN 2 of 1892.
67. *AGRCD* 1881-82, para 33.
68. The returns of criminal cases connected with emigration for the quarters ending 31 March and 30 September 1898 submitted by the Commissioners of Burdwan, Presidency, Patna, Bhagalpur and Chotanagpur Division, para 4, GD, Emigration, Resolution No. 2200, 15 July 1898, FL, CNX Quarterly Returns, FN 2 of 1898.
69. GD, Inland Emigration, Resolution dated 29 June 1891, para 8, FL, CN II Emigration, FN 3 of 1891.
70. Memorandum regarding recruiting, p. 1.
71. Letter from Dy. Commissioner, Singhbhum to the Commissioner, Chotanagpur Division, No. 80J 25/29.2.92, paras 3-7, Annual Report on the accommodation etc. provided for emigration FL, CN II Emigration, FN 2 of 1892.
72. Subsidiary orders in connection with the Report on Labour Immigration into Assam for the year 1894, Circular No. 4R, 22 Jannuary 1896, para 15, Enquiry regarding Emigrants, FL, CN IX Emigration, FN 6.
73. Buckland to the Secy. to the Government of India, Revenue and Agricultural Department, para 6.
74. Hignell, *The Administration of the Lower Provinces of Bengal*, para 44.
75. GD, Emigration, Resolution No. 1 18 July 1887, para 2, FL, CN II Emigration, FN 1 of 1887.
76. GD, Emigration, Resolution No. 1913, 30 June 1892, para 9, FL, CN II Emigration, FN 2 of 1892.
77. T.W. Holderness, Secy. to the Government of India. Revenue and Agricultural Department to the Secy. Government of Bengal, GD No. 802/39-2, 8 June 1900, Report on the result of inspection of the accommodations for free emigrants, FL, CN IV AR, FN 18 of 1900.
78. Memorandum regarding recruiting, p. 1. The average wage of non-act coolies was higher than those under the act. But their wages remained more or less stagnant. Mohapatra, '*Collies and Colliers*', p. 258. It may be pointed out that pay structure marginally varied. Under Act 1865 the wage was Rs.

5, for men and Rs. 4 for women under a three-year contract. Later the contract period became five years with the provision for an increase of Re. 1 over the last two years. In 1893, the term of contract was reduced to four years. Behal and Mohapatra, 'Tea and Money', pp. 146, 149.

79. LRAR 1906-7, DC's Office, GD, RD; CN XI Returns, FN 12, Appendix XXIX.
80. This might have been the initial feeling but they found their actual earning shrinking because of the high price of rice at their work-place. Behal and Mohapatra, 'Tea and Money', p. 157.
81. TS, Application of Damura Ho, FL, Case N. 371 of 1901-2, pp. 1–6, Gumria, FS 5, CS, VN 608, Tanaza Papers of Gotsereng, p. 7, VN 35.
82. CS, Village Note and Enquiry of Records of Right, Darposhi, p. 5, FS, A Miscellaneous, VN 652.
83. CS, Form of order sheet, Court of Settlement Officer, Land Dispute Suit No. 65 of 1895-6, pp. 31-2, Diliamarcha, FS, A Misc., VN 84.
84. CS, Petition of Kisto Tamaria, FL, Case No. 265 of 1905-6, pp. 1–9, Suamba, FS 4, VN 734.
85. CS, Bagun Jarika's Report, FL, Papers regarding Dikus of Jagannathpur, p. 5, Jagannathpur, FS 49, VN 660.
86. CS, Ejection of Sohrai Tamaria, FL, Misc. Case No. 44 of 1911, pp. 1–3, Siringsia, FS 15, VN 222.
87. CS, Eviction case arising out of criminal complaints, FL, Misc. Case No. 637 of 1908-9, pp. 1–14, Goira, FS 22, VN 139.
88. The job of an arkatti was lucrative. His per coolie earning which was Rs. 5 in 1877 rose to Rs.10 in 1883 and Rs. 20 in 1888. Behal and Mohapatra, 'Tea and Money', p. 153.
89. TS, *Tanaza* Papers of Udajo, pp. 3-4, VN 70.
90. TS, *Tanaza* Papers of Kharband, pp. 5-6, VN 33.
91. DR of *elaka* of Tusa Manki, FL, R/1022 of 1912-13, Misc. Case No. 434 of 1911-2, p. 8; DR R/126, pp. 13–5.
92. CS, Report of *elaka* of Ghono Manki of Sindurigauri, FL, Misc. Case No. 2040 of 1909-10, Jaipur, FS 3, VN 620.
93. DR of Turam Manki's *elaka*, FL, R/1018 of 1912-3, Misc. Case No. 324 of 1912-3, p. 3.
94. DR of the *elaka* of Joseph Manki, FL, R/754 of 1911-2, Misc. Case No. 435 of 1911-2, p. 2; DR of the *elaka* of Gangaram Manki, FL, R/627 of 1912-3, Misc. Case No. 600 of 1911-2, p. 10; DR, R/1024, pp. 3, 38, DR, R/995, p. 5.
95. Application of Damura Ho.
96. CS, Case between Bonga Ho and Ganga Naik, FL, Misc. Case No. 646 of 1910-11, pp. 1-6, Deogaon, VN 626.
97. TS, *Tanaza* Papers of Gumuria, pp. 4-5, VN, 45.
98. TS, Cases under section 86 of Purda, Case No. 41/86 of 1917, p. 2, VN 28.
99. Dalton, *Tribal History*, p. 191.

100. Ibid., pp. 194, 206.
101. Tickell, 'Memoir', pp. 804-6.
102. Ibid., p. 807; Dalton, *Tribal History*, pp. 205–6.
103. Eviction case arising out of criminal complaints.
104. DR of *elaka* of Gardi Manki, FL, R/625 of 1912-3, Misc. Case No. 545 of 1911-2, p. 4; DR, R/1024, p. 39; DR, R/126, pp. 20–1.
105. Order of Mr. Thomson, Deputy Commissioner of Singhbhum regarding the exclusion of Dikus and prohibition of transfer of lands to Dikus, Standing Order Book, pp. 73-4; Kolhan Standing Order of L.B. Burrows, Kolhan Deputy Collector, 6 March 1909, Standing Order Book, p. 170.
106. CS, Ejection of Sohrai Tamaria, Abin Manki of Khairpal' a Report, pp. 2–8, FL, Misc. Case No. 10 of 1907-8, Khairpal, VN 540.

Glossary

Abkari	Excise department.
Adivasi	Autochthonous people, designated as the Scheduled Tribe.
Andi	A form of settled marriage among the Hos.
Apartipi	A form of love marriage among the Hos.
Anna	One-sixteenth of a rupee.
Arkati	Decoy, recruiter of labour for plantation etc.
Asan	Terminalia tomontosa.
Bad	Second class of rice land for wet cultivation.
Bandh	An embankment made at the lower end of a depression or by embanking three sides of a slope.
Bera	First class of rice land for wet cultivation.
Bigha	A measure of land varying in extent. In Bengal it contained only 1600 square yards or a little less than one-third of an acre.
Bonga	Spirit.
Bhuinhar	Original Munda settler.
Challan	Despatch.
Chaprasi	A messenger or courier.
Chatak	One-sixteenth of a seer.
Conchu	Potter.
Deshi	Belonging to or born in a country, a native of a country.
Deuri	A village priest.
Diku	Outsider, more often a non-*Adivasi*.
Dhur	A measure of land, one-twentieth part of a *katha*.
Ghee	A clarified milk butter.
Gitiora	Dormitory system of education and training.
Golmal	Disturbance.
Gonong	Bride-price.
Gora	Cultivated upland.

Gowala	Cowherd.
Haga	Agnates.
Hakuknama	Record of Rights issued to a Manki or Munda.
Hal	Plough.
Ham	Old man, village founder.
Handia	Rice beer.
Hat	Market place, weekly market.
Hatu	Village.
Huring	Junior or non-founding killi.
Jahera	Sacred grove.
Jangtopa	Burial of the bones of a dead man.
Jat	Caste.
Jote	Tenure of a cultivator.
Jungle	Forests.
Kaji	Language.
Kamhar	Blacksmith.
Kanungo	Village and district revenue officers.
Katha	A measure of land, the twentieth part of a Bengal *bigha* i.e. 80 sq. yards.
Khash	Private.
Khazanchi	A treasurer, a cash-keeper.
Khet	A piece of agricultural land.
Khuntkatti	Original clearance.
Khuntkattidar	Original clearer of land in a village.
Killedar	Commandant or holder of a fort.
Killi	Clan or sept among the Hos, *Adivasis*.
Kos	A measure of distance varying in different parts of India, usually two miles.
Kumhar	Potter.
Kusum	Schleichera trijuga.
Lakhiraj	Holder of a revenue-free grant of village.
Lakhirajdar	Holder of a revenue-free grant.
Larka	Fighting
Ma-Bap	Mother-father.
Mahali	Sweeper or musician tribe.
Mahua	Bassia latifolia.
Mallah	Fisherman.
Manki	Head of a *pir*.
Marang	Senior, founding killi.
Matkum	Middle meaning the Bhumij.

Munda	Head of a village.
Noukrana	Service tenure.
Pachai	An intoxicating drink prepared from the fermentation of rice or other grains.
Pahun/Pahan	Village priest.
Parcha	Settlement record.
Purdah	Screen, curtain.
Parwana	Summons, warrant.
Paseri	A weight of five seers.
Pathsala	A village school.
Pir	A cluster of villages resembling a *pargana*.
Praja	Subject.
Raiyat	Tenant cultivator.
Ramtila	Ramtiya in Ho, oil-producing plant grown on *gora* land.
Rajikhusi	A form of love marriage among the Hos.
Sag	Spinach.
Sahukar	Moneylender.
Sal	Shorea robusta.
Saligram-sila	Black fossil ammonite.
Saptapadi	Going seven paces together by the bride and groom round the sacred fire lit during Hindu marriage.
Sardar	Leader of the recruiters of labour.
Sardari	The act of such recruitment.
Sasandiri	A gravestone placed flat over the burial bones in a *sasan* i.e. burial place.
Seer	Measure of weight, one-fortieth of a maund.
Selamee	A tribute.
Sepahi	Sepoy.
Sindurdan	Painting the forehead of the bride with vermilion during Hindu marriage.
Singbonga	Sun god.
Surmi-durmi	Sarak tanks.
Tal-pat	Palm-leaf.
Taluk	Subdivision of a district, landed estate.
Thana	Police station.
Thika	Mortgage.
Ulgulan	Uprising.

Bibliography

PRIMARY SOURCES

A. Government Records—Manuscripts and Reports

Bihar State Archives

Manuscripts

South West Frontier Political Despatch Register.
Vol. 26 from 6 October 1819 to 10 November 1820.
Vol. 27 from 20 April 1820 to 7 June 1821.
Vol. 231 from 13 May 1837 to 1 December 1840.

Printed

Amendment of the Chotanagpur Tenancy Act with special reference to the Kolhan Government Estate, Singhbhum, Government of Bihar and Orissa, Revenue Department, File No. IIT-26 of 1931, Nos. 39 and 40

Commissioner's Record Room and Library, Ranchi

Printed

Annual General Administration Report, Chotanagpur Division, 1886-7.

Proceedings of the Government of Bengal, General Department Miscellaneous, November 1987, File No. 155, File Serial 1-3.

Proceedings of the Government of Bengal, General Department Miscellaneous, April 1911, Quinquennial Administration Report of the Chota Nagpur Division for the period ending the 31st March 1910, File 5-R/6, Nos. 11-12.

District Record Room, Chaibasa

Manuscripts

Acquisition of Land in Kurta Village by Messrs T.I. Steel Company.
Appointment, Leave and Transfer of the Kanungo.
Craven Settlement Village Papers.
Detailed List of Permanent Establishment.
Diku Report.
Emigration Papers.
Excise Department Papers.
Forest Department Papers.
General Administration Report, 1878-9, 1883-4.
Land Revenue Administration Reports, Singhbhum.
Note on the History of Singhbhum during the decade 1910-11.
Registers of Criminal Cases.
Standing Order Book.
Tuckey Settlement Village Papers comprising.
  Khuntkatti Papers.
  Records of cases u/s 83, 85.
  Tanaza Papers.
  Village Notes.

Oriental and India Office Collections (OIOC)

Extract Political Letter from Bengal, 9 May 1823, F/4 800/21438 Bengal Political Department.
Extract Bengal Political Consultations, No. 106, 15 April 1820.
Extract Bengal Political Consultations, No. 38, 3 June 1820.

West Bengal State Archives

Judicial Proceedings, Judicial Department, May 1864, Proceedings 30-1.
Revenue Department, Proceeding No. 122, June 1867.
Revenue Department, File No. 16-S/2, Nos. 113-14, 116-7.

Reports/Gazetteers

Craven, J.A. *Final Report on the Settlement of the Kolhan Government Estate* 1897, (Calcutta, 1898).

Hignell, S.R. (Compiler), *The Administration of the Lower Provinces of Bengal during the Lieutenant Governorship of Sir John Woodburn, being a supplement to Annual General Administration Report for 1901-02*, Bengal Secretariat Press, (Calcutta, 1903).

McAlpin, M.C. *Report on the condition of the Sonthals in the Districts of Birbhum, Bankura, Midnapore and North Balasore*, (Calcutta, 1981), (1909).

McPherson, T.S. *Final Report on the operations for the preparation of a record of rights in Pargana Porahat, district of Singhbhum 1905-7*, (Calcutta, 1906).

O'Malley, L.S.S. *Bengal District Gazetteers Singhbhum, Seraikela and Kharsawan*, The Bengal Secretariat Book Depot, (Calcutta, 1910).

Prasad, C.B. *Final Report on Survey and Settlement Operations in the District of Singhbhum 1958-1965*, Secretariat Press, (Patna, 1970).

Reid, J. *Final Report on the Survey and Settlement Operations in the District of Ranchi 1902-1910*, Bengal Secretariat Book Depot, (Calcutta, 1912).

Ricketts, H. (ed.), *Report on the district of Singhbhum. Selection from the Records of the Bengal Government*, No. XVI, (Calcutta, 1854).

Roy Choudhury, P.C. *Bihar District Gazetteers Singhbhum*, Superintendent. Secretariat Press, (Patna, 1958).

Tuckey, A.D. *Final Report on the Resettlement of the Kolhan Government Estate in the District of Singhbhum 1913-1918*, Superintendent, Government Printing, Bihar and Orissa, (Patna, 1920).

B. Private Collections

Bihar and Orissa DO No. 2673, 2708PR. Ranchi, 10 September 1930.

Sanad to Babu Ratneshvar Roy, 1 January 1930.

Tour Diary of Ratneshvar Roy.

SECONDARY SOURCES

Published

Archer, W.G. *Tribal Law and Justice: A Report on the Santal*, Concept Publishing Company Pvt. Ltd., (New Delhi, 1984).

Archer, W.G. and Datta, B.K. *Ho Durang: a Ho Song Book*, (Patna, 1942).

Areeparampil, M. 'Forest Policy and Denial of Tribal Rights', in W. Fernandes (ed.), *National Development and Tribal Deprivation*. Indian Social Institute, (New Delhi, 1992).

Areeparampil, M. 'Socio-cultural and Religious Movements among the Ho Tribals of Singhbhum District of Bihar', in M. Miri (ed.), *Continuity and Change in Tribal Society*, Indian Institute of Advanced Study, (Shimla, 1993).

Areeparampil, M. 'Industries, Mines and Dispossession of Indigenous Peoples: The case of Chotanagpur', in W. Fernandes and E. Ganguly Thukral (ed.), *Development, Displacement and Rehabilitation*, *Indian Social Scientist,* (1989).

Baden-Powell, B.H. *The Indian Village Community*, Cosmo Publications, (Delhi, 1972).

Banerjee, Prathama, *Politics of Time: 'Primitives' and History-writing in a Colonial Society*, Oxford University Press (OUP), (New Delhi, 2006).

Bates, C. and Carter, M. 'Tribal Migration in India and Beyond' in Gyan Prakash (ed.), *The World of the Rural Labourer in Colonial India,* OUP, (Delhi, 1994), (1992).

Bates, C. and Carter, M. 'Tribal and Indentured Migrants in Colonial India: Modes of Recruitment and Forms of Incorporation', in Robb, P (ed.). *Dalit Movements and the Meanings of Labour in India,* OUP, (Delhi, 1999), (1993).

Behal, R.P. and Mohapatra, P.P. 'Tea and Money versus Human Life: The Rise and Fall of the Indenture System in the Assam Tea Plantation 1840-1908', *The Journal of Peasant Studies*, Vol. 19, No. 1, (October 1991).

Beteille, Andre 'The Concept of Tribe with Special Reference to India' in Andre Beteille (ed.), *Society and Politics in India: Essays in Comparative Perspective,* OUP, (Delhi, 1992).

Bhadra, G. 'Four Rebels of Eighteen-Fifty Seven', in *Subaltern Studies IV*, OUP, (Delhi, 1990), (1985).

Bodding, P.O. 'Some Remarks on the Position of Women among the Santals', in J. Troisi (ed.), *The Santals: A Collection of Readings*, vol. 6, (New Delhi, 1979).

Bodding, P.O. (Tr.), *Traditions and Institutions of the Santals/ Horkoren Mare Hapramko Raek Katha,* Bahumukhi Prakashan, Indian Reprint, (New Delhi, 1994).

Bose, N.K. *Tribal Life in India*, National Book Trust, India, (New Delhi, 1980), (1971).

Bradley-Birt, F.B. *Chota Nagpore: A Little Known Province of the Empire*, (London, 1903).

Breman, J. *Of Peasants, Migrants and Paupers*, OUP, (Delhi, 1985).

Carr, E.H. *What is History*, Penguin Books, (1961).

Carrin-Bouez, M. 'Rethinking Female Participation in Tribal Labour in Chotanagpur and Bengal', in Robb, P. (ed.). *Dalit Movements and the Meanings of Labour in India,* OUP, (Delhi, 1999), (1993).

Chakravorty Spivak (tr.), G. *Of Grammatology by Jaqcues Derrida*, Motilal Banarsidass, (Delhi, 1994) (1976).

Chakravarty, L. 'Emergence of an Industrial Labour Force in a Dual Economy—British India, 1880-1920', *The Indian Economic and Social History Review,* Vol. XV, No. 3, (July-September 1978).

Chaudhuri, B.B. Auponiveshik Purbabharate Hindu Adivasi Sanskritik Samparka', *Chaturanga,* (Magh 1401, Jaistha 1402, Bhadra 1403, Pous 1403, Shravan-Ashwin 1404).

Chaudhuri, B.B. 'Tribal Society in Transition: Eastern India, 1787-1920' in M. Hasan and N. Gupta (ed.), *India's Colonial Encounter: Essays in Memory of Eric Stokes*, Manohar, (Delhi, 1993).

Cohn, B.S. *Colonialism and its forms of Knowledge*, OUP, (Delhi, 1997).

Dalton, E.T. *Tribal History of Eastern India* (original title *Descriptive Ethnology of Bengal*), Cosmo Publication, (Delhi, 1973), (1872).

Damodaran, Vinita 'Indigenous Forests: Discourse, and Resistance in Chotanagpur, 1860-2002', in G. Cederlof and K. Sivaramakrishnan (eds.), *Ecological Nationalisms: Nature, Livelihoods, and Identities in South Asia*, Permanent Black, (Delhi, 2005).

——. "Colonial Constructions of the 'Tribe' in India: The Case of Chotanagpur", *The Indian Historical Review*, XXXIII, I, (January 2006).

Dasgupta, P.K. 'The Adi Samaj Movement among the Ho', in K.S.

Singh (ed.), *Tribal Situation in India*, Indian Institute of Advanced Study, (Shimla, 1972).

Dasgupta, Sangeeta 'From 'Description' to 'Definition': Mapping the Oraons and the 'tribe' in Chotanagpur'. Paper presented at St. Antony's College, (Oxford, May 2007).

Das Gupta, Sanjukta 'The Changing World of the Singhbhum Hos, 1820-1932', *The Indian Historical Review*, XXXIII, I, (January 2006).

——'Rebellion in a Little Known District of the Empire', in Sabyasachi Bhattacharya (ed.) *Rethinking 1857*, Orient Longman, (New Delhi, 2007).

Dasgupta, S. 'Adivasi Politics in Midnapur, c. 1760-1924', *Subaltern Studies IV*, OUP, (Delhi, 1990), (1985).

Datta, K.K. *The Santal Insurrection of 1855-57,* University of Calcutta Press, (Calcutta, 1940).

Datta, K.K. (ed.), *Unrest Against British Rule in Bihar 1831-1859,* (Patna, 1957).

Datta, S.N. *The Chotanagpur Tenancy Act*, (Bengal Act VI of 108), (Patna, 1928).

Dube, S.C. (ed.) *Tribal Heritage of India*, Vol. I, Vikas Publishing House Pvt. Ltd., (New Delhi, 1977).

Dunbar, W. 'Some Observations on the Manners, Customs, and Religious Opinions of the Lurka Coles', *Journal of the Asiatic Society of Great Britain and Northern Ireland*, Vol. 18, (1861).

Eagleton, T. *Literary Theory,* Basil Blackwell, (Oxford, 1990), (1983).

Engels, D. 'The Myth of the Family Unit: *Adivasi* Women in Coal Mines and Tea Plantations in early Twentieth-Century Bengal', in Robb, P. (ed.). *Dalit Movements and the Meanings of Labour in India,* OUP, (Delhi, 1999) (1993).

Fuchs, S. *Rebellious Prophets: A Study of Messianic Movements in Indian Religions*, Asia Publishing House, (Bombay, 1965).

Ginzburg, C. *The Cheese and the Worms: The Cosmos of a Sixteenth-Century Miller*, Routledge and Kegan Paul, (London and Henley, 1980).

Ghosh, K. 'A Market for Aboriginality: Primitivism and Race Classification in the Indentured Labour Market of Colonial India' in Bhadra, G., Gyan Prakash and Tharu, S (ed.), *Subaltern Studies X*, OUP, (Delhi, 2000), (1999).

Ghurye, G.S. *The Scheduled Tribes* (original title *The Aborigines so called and Their Future*), Popular Prakashan, (Bombay, 1995), (1943).

Guha, R. *Elementary Aspects of Peasant Insurgency in Colonial India*, OUP, (Delhi, 1983).

Guha, R. 'The Prose of Counter-Insurgency', *Subaltern Studies II*, OUP, (Delhi, 1986), (1983).

Guha, R. *History at the Limit of World-History,* OUP, (New Delhi, 2002).

Guha, S. 'Lower Strata, Older Races, and Aboriginal Peoples: Racial Anthropology and Mythical History Past and Present', *The Journal of Asian Studies* 57, No. 2, (May 1998).

Hagen, J.R. and Yang, A. "A. Local Source for the Study of Rural India: The 'Village Notes' of Bihar", *The Indian Economic and Social History Review*, Vol. XIII, No. 1 (January-March, 1976).

Hardiman, D. *The Coming of the Devi: The Adivasi Assertion in Western India*, OUP, (Delhi, 1987).

Hembram, P.C. 'Return to the Sacred Grove', in K.S. Singh (ed.), *Tribal Movements in India*, Vol. 2, Manohar, (Delhi, 1983).

Heredia, R.C. 'Tribal History: Living Word or Dead Letter?', *Economic and Political Weekly*, Vol. AXE, No. 18, (April 29-May 5, 2000).

Hospers, J. *An Introduction to Philosophical Analysis*, Allied Publishers, (New Delhi, 1997).

Hunter, W.W. *A Statistical Account of Bengal*, Vol. XVII, Concept Publishing Company Pvt. Ltd., (Delhi, 1976), (1877).

Jha, J.C. *Kol Insurrection in Chotanagpur*, (Calcutta, 1964).

—— *The Tribal Revolt of Chotanagpur* (*1831-32*), K.P. Jayaswal Research Institute, (Patna, 1987).

Kelkar, G. and Nathan, D. 'Women's Land Rights and Witches', in M. Miri (ed.), *Continuity and Change in Tribal Society*, Indian Institute of Advanced Study, (Shimla, 1993)

Kishwar, M 'Toilng without Rights: Ho Women in Singhbhum', *Economic and Political Weekly*, (17, 24, 31 January 1987).

Kosambi, D.D. *An Introduction to the Study of Indian History*, Popular Prakashan, (Bombay, 1985).

Le Goff, L. *History and Memory*, Columbia University Press, (New York, 1992).

Majumdar, D.N. *A Tribe in Transition: Study in Cultural Pattern*, Longmans Green and Co. Ltd., (Calcutta, 1937).

—— *The Affairs of a Tribe*, (Calcutta, 1950).

Mohapatra, P.P. 'Coolies and Colliers: A Study of the Agrarian Context of Labour Migration from Chotanagpur, 1880-1920', *Studies in History,* 1, 2, n.s. (1985).

—— 'Land and Credit Market in Chotanagpur 1880-1950', *Studies in History,* 6.2. n.s., (1990).

—— 'Class Conflict and Agrarian regimes in Chotanagpur 1860-1950', *The Economic and Social History Review*, 28, 1 (1991).

Norris, C. *Deconstruction, Theory and Practice*, Routledge, (London and New York, 1993), (1982).

Patna Law Journal Reports, 1996 (2), October, Part 10, November, Part 11, Malhotra Books, (Patna, 1996).

Paty, C.K. *History of Seraikela and Kharsawan States* (*1620-1956 AD*), Concept Publishing Company Pvt. Ltd., (New Delhi, 2002).

——(ed.) *Forest, Government and Tribe*, Concept Publishing Company Pvt. Ltd., (New Delhi, 2006).

Risley, H.H. *The Tribes and Castes of Bengal*, Vol. I, (Calcutta, 1981), (1891).

Rosaldo, R. *Ilongot Headhunting 1883-1974: A Study in Society and History*, Stanford University Press, Stanford, (California, 1980).

Roy, S.C. *The Mundas and their Country*, Asia Publishing House, (Calcutta, 1970).

—— *Oraon Religion and Customs*, Edition Indian, (Calcutta, 1972), (1928).

Roy Choudhury, P.C. *1857 in Bihar* (*Chotanagpur and Santhal Parganas*), (Patna, 1959), (1957).

Sahu, M. *The Kolhan under the British Rule,* (Calcutta, 1985).

Said, E.W. *Orientalism*, Penguin Books, (1985).

—— *Culture and Imperialism*, Vintage, (London, 1994), (1993).

Samaddar, R. *Memory, Identity, Power: Politics in the Jungle Mahals* (*West Bengal*), *1890-1950*, Sangam Books, (London, 1998).

Sarkar, T. 'Jitu Santal's Movement in Malda, 1924-1932: A Study in Tribal Protest', *Subaltern Studies IV*, OUP, (Delhi, 1990), (1985).

Sen, A.K. 'Raisaheb Ratneshvar Rayer Sarkari Safarnama O Sighbhum 1927-30', *Aitihasik,* Vol. 5, No 1, (Kartik-Chaitra, 1402 BS).

—— *Wilkinson's Rules: Context, Content and Ramifications,* Tata College, (Chaibasa, 1999).

—— 'Writing Local History and the District Record Room.' Proceedings of the Indian Historical Records Commission, 58th Session, (2003).

——'Conceptualization of the Hos of Singhbhum as a Tribe', in P. Sen (ed.), *Changing Tribal Life: A Socio-Philosophical Perspective*, Concept Publishing Company Pvt. Ltd., (New Delhi, 2003).

——'Tribe-Peasant-Tribe Continuum: The Dynamics of Ho Identity', in S. Gopal (ed.), *Colonial India: A Centenary Tribute to Professor K.K. Datta*, Research Publication Series-4, Veer Kunwar Singh University, (Arrah, 2006).

——'Constructing a Different World: Pages from the Diary of Raisaheb Sashi Bhusan Sarkar' *Manwa Katha*, Vol. I, No. I, (October 2007).

——'Collective Memory and Reconstruction of Ho History', *Indian Folklore Research Journal*, Vol. 5, No. 8, (December 2008).

Sen, S.K. *Tribal Struggle for Freedom: Singhbhum1820-1858*, Concept Publishing Company Pvt. Ltd., (New Delhi, 2008).

Sherwin, D. 'The Control of Land and Labour in Chota Nagpur, 1858-1908' in D. Rothermund and D.C. Wadhwa (eds.), *Zamindars, Mines and Peasants*, Manohar, (Delhi, 1978).

Singh, C.P. *The Ho Tribe of Singhbhum,* Classical Publications, (New Delhi, 1978).

Singh, K.S. 'State-Formation in Tribal Society: Some Preliminary Observations', *Journal of Indian Anthropological Society*, Vol. 6, (1971).

——'The Munda Land System and Revenue Reforms in Chotanagpur during 1869-1908' vide R.S. Sharma (ed.), *Land Revenue in India: Historical Studies*, Motilal Banarsidass, (Patna, 1971).

——(ed.), *Tribal Situation in India*, Indian Institute of Advanced Study, (Shimla, 1972).

——*Tribal Society in India: An Anthropo-historical Perspective*, Manohar, (Delhi, 1985).

Singhdeo, T.N.N. *Singhbhum, Seraikela and Kharsawan—Through the Ages*, (Calcutta, No date).

Sinha, S. 'State Formation and Rajput Myth in Tribal Central India', *Man in India*, Vol. 42, No. I, (March, 1962).

——'Tribe, Caste and Peasant Continua', *Man in India*, Vol. 45, No. I, (March 1965).

——(ed.), *Tribal Politics and State Systems in Pre Colonial Eastern and North Eastern India*, K.P. Bagchi, (Calcutta, 1987).

Sinha, S.C., Sen, J. and Panchabhai, S. 'The Concept of Diku among the Tribes of Chotanagpur', *Man in India*, Vol. 49, No. 2, (April-June 1969).

Sinha, S.S. "Adivasis, Gender and the 'Evil Eye': The Construction(s) of Witches in Colonial Chotanagpur", in *The Indian Historical Review,* Volume XXXIII, Number 1, (January 2006).

Sivaramakrishnan, K. *Modern Forests: Statemaking and Environmental Changes in Colonial Eastern India*, OUP, (Delhi, 1999).

Skaria, A. 'Writing, Orality and Power in the Dangs, Western India, 1800s-1920s', *Subaltern Studies IX*, OUP, (Delhi, 1997).

Skaria, A. *Hybrid Histories: Frontiers and Wildness in Western India*, OUP, (Delhi, 1999).

Smith, R.S. 'Rule-by-records and rule-by-reports: complementary aspects of the British imperial rule of law', *Contributions to Indian Sociology* (n.s.) 19, 1, (1985).

Spivak, G.C. *Jacques Derrida of Grammatology*, Motilal Banarsidass, (Delhi, 1994), (1976).

Srivastava, A.K. *Coal Mining Industry in India*, (New Delhi, 1988).

Sturrock, J. *Structuralism and Since from Levi Stauss to Derrida*, OUP, (Oxford, 1988), (1979).

Sur, N. 'Chotanagpur and the Rising of 1857', *Bengal: Past and Present*, (January-December 1986).

Tharu, S. and Niranjana, T. 'Problems for a Contemporary Theory of Gender'. *Subaltern Studies X*, OUP, 1999, (1996).

Tickell, Lt. S.R. 'Memoir on the Ho desum' (improperly called Kolehan)', *Journal of Asiatic Society of Bengal*, vol. XI, part II, (1840).

——'Vocabulary of the Ho language', *Journal of the Asiatic Society of Bengal*, vol. IX, part II, July to December 1840, New Series, (Calcutta, 1840).

White, H. *Tropics of Discourse: Essays in Cultural Criticism*. The Johns Hopkins University Press, (Baltimore and London, 1987).

Unpublished

Bosu Mullick, S. 'Changes in Gender Relations and the Question of Witches'.

Mahto, D.N. 'Geomorphology of the Kharkai Basin', Ranchi University Ph. D. Thesis, (May 1998).

Sen, A.K. *From Village Elder to British Judge: Custom, Customary Law and Tribal Society*.

——'Differential Peasantisation and the Changing Socio-Economy of the Ho Tribe of Singhbhum', presented at the Seminar on the Changing Scenario of the Tribals and Indigenous People of Jharkhand, Bihar, West Bengal and Orissa, *The Asiatic Society*, Calcutta, (8 January 2003).

——'Contesting Marginalization: Colonial Representation of the Indigenes in the Great Rebellion of 1857-58', presented at the *International Conference on Contesting Identities: Tribes, Indigenous Peoples and Adivasis in Colonial and Postcolonial India*, organised by Department of History, Visva Bharati, Santiniketan, (26-27 November, 2005).

——'Collaboration and Conflict: Environmental Legacies of the Ho of Kolhan during 1700-1918', in Deepak Kumar, Vinita Damodaran and Rohan D'Souza (eds.), *The British Empire and the Natural World: Environmental Encounters in South Asia*, OUP, New Delhi, (Forthcoming).

——'Water bodies, Changing Social Ecology and Ho *Adivasis* of Colonial Singhbhum'.

——'Redefining Archaeology and the ethno-history of pre-colonial Singhbhum, presented at the International Seminar on *Applications of Anthropological Researches in Human Life* organized by *The Asiatic Society*, Calcutta, (7, 8, 9 January 2009).

Yorke, M.P. 'Decisions and Analogy: Political Structure and Discourse among the Ho Tribals of India', Ph. D. Thesis, The School of Oriental and African Studies, University of London, (October 1976).

Index